The Ultimate Training System

Steven J. Fleck, Ph.D.

William J. Kraemer, Ph.D.

Advanced Research Press
New York, 1996

For information contact: Advanced Research Press, 2120 Smithtown Avenue, Ronkonkoma, NY 11779

F I R S T   E D I T I O N

Library of Congress Cataloging-in-Publication Data
Steven Fleck, Ph.D.,
William Kraemer, Ph.D,
Periodization Breakthrough!

1. Exercise. 2. Physical Fitness. 3. Strength.
I. Title.
Library of Congress Catalog Number: 96-85249
ISBN 1-889462-00-4 (hardcover)

Printed in the United States of America

Published by: Advanced Research Press, Inc.

                                   2120 Smithtown Ave.

                                   Ronkonkoma, NY 11779

Publisher/President: Steve Blechman

Project Director: Roy Ulin

Design Director: Edmund Passarelli - Body Comp, Inc.

Assistant Art Directors: Marc Passarelli
                                   May Egner

Copy Editing: Mag Pro, Inc.
                                   Alan Paul
                                   Robert McCann

Illustrations: Kevin Newman

Printed by: R.R. Donnelley & Sons

ACKNOWLEDGMENTS

We would first like to thank our many colleagues and friends who have been a source of unyielding support for the endeavors we have undertaken over the years. We are fortunate to have been part of an exciting time in the history of strength training, one in which the underlying laboratory study of such training has increased dramatically. Laboratory research around the world has produced more studies in the scientific/medical literature during the past 15 years than in all of the previous years combined. However, we still have a long way to go in our efforts to get this data into the hands of people like you who desire to utilize the best available information to meet your training goals. To this end, we have dedicated our careers.

We would especially like to thank Mr. Steve Blechman for his support of this noble endeavor to help educate the public with the best available information. His encouragement and support have made this project possible. To Mr. Roy Ulin for his comprehensive approach to putting the best possible book on periodization together, we thank you for your tireless efforts. To Mr. Alan Paul for leading a super team of copy editors, particularly Mr. Bob McCann, and for working so hard to make the book work, we thank you. To Mr. Ed Passarelli and his team of artists for the creative artistic innovations that make this book fun to read, we thank you. To Ms. Joann Ruble and Ms. Carol Gardner for their tireless typing of draft upon draft of the manuscript, we thank you.

And to the many graduate students at Penn State University who have supported a lively discussion of the science of resistance training over the years, helping to formulate thoughts and ideas, we thank you.

Finally, to our families and close friends who have supported each of us over the years and helped us to grow, we thank you, as we know it has not always been easy.

As readers, we hope this book will challenge you to think, using your minds to design a resistance training program that will reach beyond the development which you may have previously thought possible. We hope this book provides a framework for your thoughts and understanding, giving you the keys to unlock your own physical potential as a human being. Each of you is a unique individual in every way and your resistance training program must meet your individual needs—for there is no one, all-encompassing, "secret" program. *Periodization Breakthrough!* speaks to the many opportunities there are to choose and decide what is right for you, as an individual. This book is dedicated to giving you all the tools you will need to control the destiny of your physical development through the employment of resistance training.

We wish you good luck and good training!

Steven J. Fleck, Ph.D. and William J. Kraemer, Ph.D.

FOREWORD

All books have a title page and a foreword. All readers agree on the desirability of a title page, but with almost equal unanimity they find the foreword needless. This foreword is similar to others in that regard.

Forewords in texts are written to introduce the author(s) and the book to the potential readers. There is no need for me to introduce the authors—they are well-known enough, even, I may say, famous in the strength training community. Drs. Steve Fleck and William Kraemer have authored several books on strength training, including such a best-seller as *Designing Resistance Training Programs*. Both of them possess a unique combination of knowledge, both scientific and applied. Dr. Fleck and Dr. Kraemer are distinguished scientists in muscle and exercise physiology and have published hundreds of papers in the scientific journals, but at the same time they are practitioners familiar with weight training for sports and fitness from their personal experiences as athletes, coaches and supervisors of strength training programs. Dr. Fleck has worked for many years as a physiologist and advisor for elite national athletes at the United States Olympic Committee's Olympic Training Center in Colorado Springs. Dr. Kraemer is a colleague of mine here at Penn State and has had extensive experience with strength training from both the practical and scientific perspectives. Dr. Kraemer was also the founding editor of the *Journal of Strength and Conditioning Research*. Hence, the book is written by real experts on the topic.

Training periodization—the process of dividing training sessions into smaller and more manageable intervals—does not need promoting. This is an essential principle of successful strength training and a popular topic of discussion among coaches and athletes. This concept is many times neglected in the sports, health and fitness literature. This book bridges the gap and provides a simple and straightforward explanation of this training concept. *Periodization Breakthrough!* is the first book written in English devoted completely to this important topic. The authors describe both the North American and European approaches to the planning of the training programs. The authors also discuss the available scientific evidence for the use of periodization in resistance training. More importantly, they provide a wealth of practical examples in an easy to understand style of presentation. They have taken what many have made a complex concept and presented it in a manner for all to use. In essence, they call upon their practical experience to make this book reader-friendly. They provide the readers with an abundance of practical advice and examples of training plans which should be of great interest whether you are a beginner or an elite athlete.

I read the book with great pleasure and benefit. I am certain that you will experience the same.

Vladimir M. Zatsiorsky, Ph.D.

Professor and Director, Biomechanics Laboratory
Penn State University

May, 1996

Dr. Zatsiorsky is a world-renowned sport biomechanist and former strength and conditioning consultant for the Soviet Union Olympic teams. He is the author of Science and Practice of Strength Training.

To Maelu, my loving wife,
Marv and Elda, my parents,

for all their support throughout my life,
and to all the coaches and athletes who have shared
their training concepts and ideas with me.

Steven Fleck

To Joan, Daniel, Anna and Maria,

for their love and support,

Bill Kraemer

Steven J. Fleck, Ph.D.

Steven J. Fleck is an internationally known expert in the area of resistance training. He is the former head of the Physical Conditioning Program for the United States Olympic Committee. He advises national and international caliber athletes on weight training. Dr. Fleck has also held academic and scientific positions at the University of Alabama at Birmingham, Ohio University and the University of North Carolina at Greensboro. Dr. Fleck received his undergraduate degree in biology and physical education from the University of Wisconsin-LaCrosse, masters and doctoral degrees from The Ohio State University in exercise physiology. He has presented at numerous international conferences, including conferences sponsored by the Spanish, Australian, Puerto Rican and New Zealand Olympic Committees. Dr. Fleck is a past Vice President of Basic and Applied Research for the National Strength and Conditioning Association and has served that association in many other capacities. In 1991 he received the Outstanding Sport Scientist Award from the National Strength and Conditioning Association. Dr. Fleck is also a Fellow of the American College of Sports Medicine. He is a member of many professional organizations and serves on numerous committees and editorial boards. Dr. Fleck has published a great many scientific articles on strength training and two prior books on strength and conditioning with Dr. Kraemer.

William J. Kraemer, Ph.D.

William J. Kraemer is the Director of Research in the Center for Sports Medicine and the Associate Director of the Center for Cell Research at the Pennsylvania State University and a Professor of Applied Physiology. He holds appointments in the Department of Kinesiology, the Intercollege Program in Physiology, the Noll Physiological Research Center, Milton S. Hershey Medical Center, and Gerontology Center at Penn State. He received his undergraduate degree at the University of Wisconsin-LaCrosse in Health Education and Physical Education. He received a masters degree in exercise physiology and his doctoral degree in physiology and biochemistry from the University of Wyoming. Dr. Kraemer has taught and coached on both the public school and college levels. He has held various scientific and academic appointments at the following institutions: the U.S. Army's Research Institute of Environmental Medicine in Natick, Massachusetts; an adjunct professor in the Department of Health Sciences at Boston University; and a joint faculty appointment in the Exercise Science Program and the Department of Physiology/Neurobiology at the University of Connecticut in Storrs, CT—prior to coming to Penn State in 1989. He is a past president of the National Strength and Conditioning Association (NSCA). He served that organization in many capacities, from chair of the Research Committee to Vice President of Basic and Applied Research. Dr. Kraemer has been honored by the NSCA with both their outstanding Sports Scientist Award in 1992 and NSCA's highest award, the Lifetime Achievement Award for his contributions to bringing science into the field of strength training. He is also a fellow in the American College of Sports Medicine. Dr. Kraemer is a member of many other professional societies and has served on numerous committees and scientific journal editorial boards. He is the current Editor-in-Chief of the *Journal of Strength and Conditioning Research*. He is also a member of the United States Olympic Committee's Science and Technology Committee. He has published over 150 scientific manuscripts and has also published two prior books on strength training with Dr. Fleck.

"Whether you are involved in bodybuilding, powerlifting, basketball, football, track, or any other competitive sport, Fleck and Kraemer show you how to use weight training scientifically to maximize your strength, power and performance. *Periodization Breakthrough!* is a no-nonsense approach to training utilizing an ever-changing variety of workouts with your body's natural cycles. It takes training out of the Dark Ages!"

—Lee Labrada

TABLE OF CONTENTS

periodized training

have you felt the frustration of never seeming to reach your training goals? Or of reaching a training plateau where progress seemed all but impossible? These typical concerns are one of the major reasons for using a long-term training plan. Periodized training, in essence, is nothing more than that—*a training plan which changes your workouts at regular intervals of time.* This systematic change generates the kind of measurable progress that leads to satisfying workouts, resulting in a greater degree of achievement in sports and an increased ability to cope with often taxing everyday physical demands.

Periodized training involves manipulating or changing training variables, such as the number of repetitions performed per set, exercises performed, the amount of weight lifted and rest periods between sets. You do not have to be a competitive bodybuilder, powerlifter or other type of athlete to benefit from periodized training—everyone can benefit from it. Peaking at just the right time—obviously of key importance to the bodybuilder and athlete—is far from the only benefit of periodized training. You will also gain in strength, power and muscular size.

Changes made in training with a periodized plan also help to keep your regimen from becoming boring. A dull training program leads to a lack of adherence and slippage into improper form, which in turn leads to jettisoning the program altogether. The next thing you know, you've given up on exercise. That won't happen with a periodized plan.

Another major reason to switch to periodized training is to prevent injuries. Were you ever at a stage in your training where you were making good gains, and continued to train intensely to the point of injury? A main reason the injury may have occurred was because you continued to push as hard as your could and your body couldn't take the stress. It was clearly time for a less intense training period, or some other change in your training which would reduce stress on your body. With periodized training, intense and less intense training periods are planned so that the stress does not accumulate to the point of adversity. In other words, rest and recovery is vital to optimal progression.

Now here's some really good news: planned intense and less intense training periods will also help prevent training plateaus. (For those who may not know, a plateau is a juncture in a training period when you are training intensely but making no gains in strength, power, muscular size, athletic performance, or any other fitness measure. All pain, no gain.) Unfortunately, when most people experience a plateau they train even more intensely. They assume they're not making gains because they're not training hard enough. This is a shame, because many times a plateau can be avoided by planning to alternate an intense training period with a less intense period. The less intense training period allows recovery from the intense one, so the body can fully recover and go on to make further progress.

You see, all gains are really made during recovery from training, at which time the body makes adaptations to the training stimulus. We can see now that recovery time is all-important—a point that will be stressed time and again in this book. In truth, it cannot be emphasized enough!

So if you are a competitive athlete, a recreational athlete, or primarily exercising for health and general fitness, there are impelling reasons to use periodized training.

In sum, planned training will help ensure continued gains, prevent injuries, keep the training from becoming boring, and help you avoid training plateaus.

WHERE DID PERIODIZED TRAINING COME FROM?

Many people credit the former Eastern Bloc countries of the Soviet Union and East Germany with developing periodized training. It was developed during the 1950s and '60s to give Eastern Bloc athletes an advantage in preparing for international competitions. Many sport scientists and coaches devoted countless hours of work to develop the concepts of periodized training to help ensure the success of the Eastern Bloc athletes in world-class, politically-tinged events like the Olympics. Actually, aspects of periodized training have also been used by some American athletes since the 1960s. This is especially true for elite swimmers, Olympic weightlifters, and track and field athletes. What was once incredibly cutting-edge training knowledge has now become an integral part of the practice of modern training.

DOES PERIODIZATION WORK?

Yes, periodization does work! No doubt about it! Myriad sport science studies have been conducted that dramatically demonstrate periodization is the real thing. Let's consider two specific studies clearly showing how periodized strength training programs result in greater gains.

High school football players training with a periodized strength training program have been compared to players using a non-periodized program (Stone et al., 1981). Both types of training were performed three times per week for six weeks. The squat, knee curl, behind-the-neck press, bench press and clean pull from the floor and from mid-thigh level were performed in both programs. After six weeks of training, the periodized program resulted in significantly greater gains in maximal squat strength for one repetition and squat strength for one repetition on a per kilogram of body weight basis. While both types of training resulted in a significant increase in vertical jump ability, periodized training significantly increased leg power during the vertical jump. Neither type of training resulted in a significant change in total body weight, probably due to the short six-week training period. Importantly, the periodized training resulted in a significant increase in lean body mass, indicating both an increase in muscle mass and a significant decrease in percent body fat.

Figure 1.1

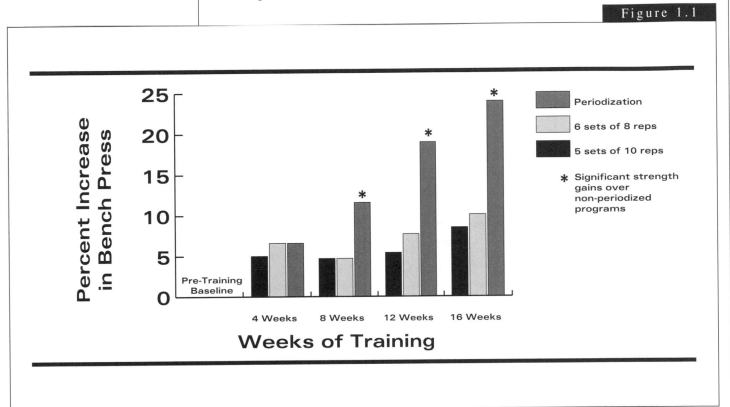

Figure 1.1. Changes in bench press maximal weight for one repetition with periodized and non-periodized programs. * = periodized program increase significantly greater than both non-periodized programs. Data from D.S. Willoughby, 1993, "The effects of mesocycle length weight training programs involving periodization and partially equated volumes on upper and lower body strength." Journal of Strength and Conditioning Research, 7(1): 2-8.

In the second study, periodization was shown to increase strength more than two different non-periodized training programs in college-age males with previous weight training experience (Willoughby, 1993). Training was performed three times per week for 16 weeks. One non-periodized program consisted of performing five sets of 10 repetitions per set at 79% of the maximal weight that could be lifted for one repetition (also called a 1 repetition maximum—1 RM). The other non-periodized program consisted of performing six sets of eight repetitions per set at 83% of the 1 RM. In the periodized program, the set and repetition scheme was changed every four weeks. Five sets of 10 repetitions per set at 79% of 1 RM were performed for the first four weeks; six sets of eight repetitions per set at 83% of 1 RM were used for the next four weeks; followed by three sets of six repetitions per set at 88% of 1 RM for yet another four weeks; and finally three sets of four repetitions per set at 92% of 1 RM for the last four weeks. Testing of 1 RM in the bench press and back squat was done every four weeks.

Figure 1.2

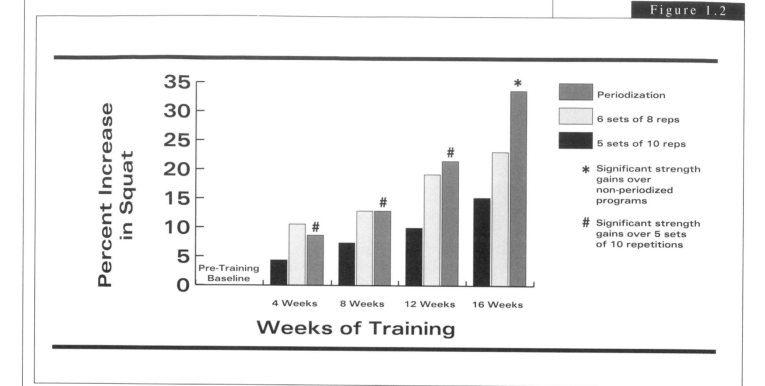

*Figure 1.2. Changes in back squat maximal weight for one repetition with periodized and non-periodized programs. # = periodized program increase significantly greater than five sets of ten repetitions program; * = periodized program increase significantly greater than both non-periodized programs. Data from D.S. Willoughby, 1993, "The effects of mesocycle length weight training programs involving periodization and partially equated volumes on upper and lower body strength." Journal of Strength and Conditioning Research, 7(1): 2-8.*

The results of the 1 RM strength tests in the back squat and bench press show that periodized training results in greater gains (Figures 1.1 and 1.2). In the bench press, after four weeks of training all three programs resulted in significant improvements in the 1 RM. However, at this stage no program resulted in gains different from any other program. But, after eight weeks of training, the periodized program resulted in significantly greater strength gains in bench press 1 RM compared to the two non-periodized programs. The periodized program also showed greater strength gains in the bench press than the two non-periodized programs after 12 and 16 weeks of training.

In the back squat, after four weeks of training the periodized program resulted in greater 1 RM strength gains than the five sets of 10 repetitions program, but not greater than the six sets of eight repetitions program. After eight and 12 weeks of training the periodized program still showed a gain in strength in the back squat greater than the five sets of ten repetitions program, but again, not greater than the six sets of eight repetitions program. However, after the full 16 weeks of training the periodized program did show an increase in back squat 1 RM strength significantly greater than both non-periodized programs. Thus, it appears periodized programs do result in strength gains greater than non-periodized programs, especially over the long haul course of time.

In the next chapter, principles of resistance training and how they relate to periodization will be discussed.

S E L E C T E D   R E A D I N G S :

• *Stone, M.H., O'Bryant, H., & Garhammer, J.G. (1981). A hypothetical model for strength training. Journal of Sports Medicine and Physical Fitness, 21, 342-351.*
• *Willoughby, D.S. (1993). The effects of mesocycle-length weight training programs involving periodization and partially equated volumes on upper and lower body strength. Journal of Strength and Conditioning Research, 7(1): 2-8.*
• *Fleck, S.J. and Kraemer, W.J. Designing Resistance Training Programs. Human Kinetics Publishers, Champaign, IL, 1987.*

training principles

nowledge of basic training principles is the first step in designing an optimal resistance training program. Such principles can be effectively applied to all manner of training programs: cardiovascular, flexibility programs or, in this case, weight training.

OVERLOAD PRINCIPLE

In order to increase muscle size and strength, the body must be stressed beyond its normal capabilities. This means that if you can bench press 150 pounds for eight repetitions, and continue to train by pressing the same amount for six reps, you'll make little or no strength gains, due to lack of sufficient stimulus. However, if you train by performing six reps with as much weight as possible, you will make some progress in bench press strength. This is because you are asking the muscles to perform more work than they are presently capable of doing, or "overloading" the muscles.

In more practical training terms, you could overload the muscles involved in the bench press by performing, say, 10 repetitions at 140 pounds for several sets, or six repetitions at 160 pounds. In other words, the overload effect can be achieved by performing more sets of the same number of repetitions at a given weight; or by attempting to perform the same number of repetitions per set at a slightly greater weight. In either case, the key is to challenge the muscles to perform more work than they can presently perform. Thus, there are many combinations of sets, repetitions and weight that might be used to overload a muscle.

In general, for weight training to lead to hypertrophy—that is, muscle growth—the resistance used should be at least 60% of the repetition maximum (1 RM) of a given exercise. If the 1 RM is 100 pounds, the repetitions must be performed with no less than 60 pounds.

Indeed, the most common way to overload a muscle during a resistance training program is to increase the weight. This means that if a program calls for performing three sets of 10 repetitions, when all three sets can be easily performed at a particular weight, it's time for the resistance to be increased slightly, thereby ensuring continued progress.

Now that we've established that programs using repetition maximum (RM) resistance ensure constant overload, let's look at the phenomenon closely. *A RM resistance is a weight that allows X but not X+1 repetitions.* So a 6 RM weight allows six but not seven repetitions per set with good exercise technique; while a 12 RM weight allows 12 but not 13 repetitions per set, and so on. Defined more succinctly, *a 1 RM is the heaviest weight that can be used for one complete repetition utilizing proper technique.* Example: if a program calls for performing four sets of six reps at a 6 RM resistance, the lifter may be able to perform six/five/five/four repetitions in each of the four sets. When a lifter can perform six repetitions in all four sets, the weight is increased slightly so it once again constitutes a 6 RM resistance.

The key point of the overload principle is that if a gain in strength, size or local muscular endurance is expected, the muscle must be asked to perform more work than it is presently capable of doing at some point during the course of the training program. It's as simple—and as complex—as that.

REST PRINCIPLE

Sufficient recovery of muscle groups between training sessions is necessary for gains in strength and muscle size to take place. Remember that: *these adaptations take place between training sessions and not during training sessions.* In fact, after a training session, due to fatigue, you are actually weaker than you were at the start of the session. In general, however, with adequate recovery between sessions, you should enter the next session at a slightly higher training level.

Given that the overload during the training sessions and the recovery between training sessions are both adequate, changes in strength before and after training should resemble an ever-increasing saw-tooth pattern (Figure 2.1). This saw-tooth pattern may also be apparent on a weekly basis. As an example, assuming you train on Monday, Wednesday and Friday, strength levels may be higher on the Monday immediately prior to your training session and after the weekend's two-day rest period. Strength levels may then decrease slightly throughout the week; but then once again, on Monday, be at a slightly higher level than the previous Monday. This pattern is all part of the body's ability to recover, grow and ultimately adapt to training demands. It's a key principle in the quest for the perfect periodization plan.

It is important to remember that adequate recovery between training sessions does not only refer to the length of time between sessions. If optimal gains in strength and muscle size are to be achieved, healthy lifestyle habits must be observed and adequate sleep must be obtained each night. Adequate sleep is a key factor because many adaptations to training occur while sleeping. In general, the length of time between training sessions for a particular muscle group should be at least 24-48 hours. If the training is very intense, longer recovery between training sessions may be necessary to ensure across-the-board gains in strength, power and muscle size.

Despite all this, one advanced training method often utilized is to not allow sufficient recovery between training sessions for a very short period of time, such as a week. This results in a very intense training week where the body's ability to recover and grow is inhibited intentionally. This is normally followed by one or two weeks of less intense training, which allows recovery from the intense week. During this less intense period, a palpable rebound in the body's adaptation to training results, leading to increased muscle size and strength.

Again, however, in general if adequate recovery is allowed between individual training sessions, the saw-tooth strength pattern will be apparent from session to session. Accordingly, if insufficient recovery time is allotted, an ever-decreasing saw-tooth pattern is apparent on a session-by-session basis—which is clearly not the long-term pattern desired if increases in strength and muscle size are the goal.

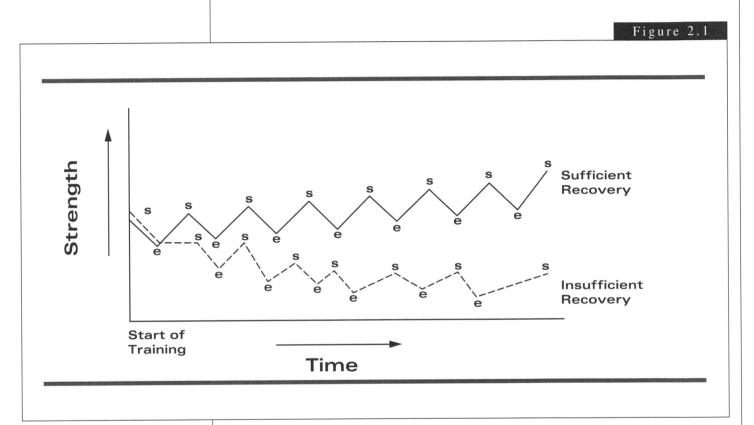

Figure 2.1

Figure 2.1. Increasing and decreasing saw-tooth pattern of strength when sufficient and insufficient recovery is allowed between training sessions. S = start of session, E = end of session.

SPECIFICITY PRINCIPLE

Simply stated, the specificity principle means training in a fashion that will bring about adaptations geared towards improving your ability at a specific activity or task. Clearly, training must be goal-related. But within that general framework, there are types of specificity that must be understood in order to optimally design a periodized weight training program.

If you are a 100-meter sprinter, for example, you will obviously want to sprint as fast as you can. But if you train only by running five miles at a relatively slow pace, you will not become a superior 100-meter sprinter any time within the next millennium or so. In fact, you may actually become slower than you are now. Are we talking waste of training time here, or what?

Let's say instead you're a powerlifter. You must aim to train with heavier weights and fewer number of repetitions—because the idea is to become good at lifting the maximal weight possible for one repetition.

The major areas of training specificity are:

Muscle Group Specificity. Here you'll train the specific muscle groups for which you desire to bring about an increase in size or strength. Leg training is great—but not when you're looking to improve your arms for specific performance needs. Focus on all relevant muscle groups to a maximally-efficient degree.

Speed Specificity. The speed or velocity at which an individual must move in order to be successful in his or her sport is an important consideration. The force velocity curve of muscle is such that if a heavy weight is to be moved as fast as possible, it will be moved at a slow velocity; whereas, if a light weight is moved as fast as possible it can be moved at a fast velocity (Figure 2.2). Most intro to physics students are already aware of the relationship between force and velocity of movement. If you are performing a 1 RM bench press, maximal forces will be developed, but the velocity of the barbell will be relatively slow. On the other hand, if you perform a repetition with 50% of your 1 RM bench press, it'll be possible to move the barbell at a relatively fast velocity. This is essentially all the force velocity curve shows.

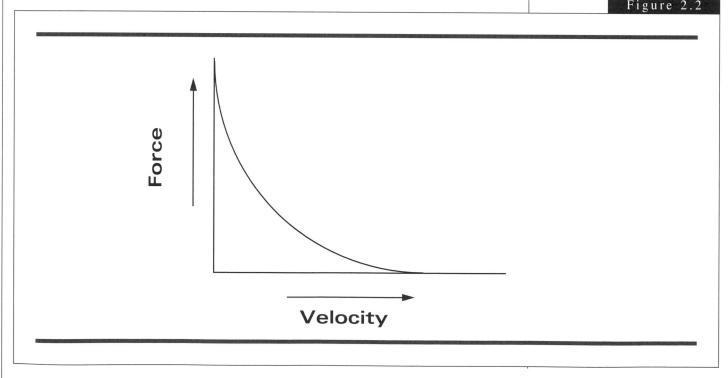

Figure 2.2

Figure 2.2. *The force velocity curve of muscle shows it is possible to move very heavy weights at only a relatively slow velocity, but that light weights can be moved at a fast velocity.*

In many sports, it is necessary to move a relatively light implement—such as a baseball, softball, or racquet—at a relatively fast velocity. Thus, congruent with the sport itself there is the indication that, at some point in training, it would be advantageous to train with lighter weights but at a faster velocity. This is the equivalent of training for power. Research indicates that although training at one velocity will result in strength increases at other velocities, velocities closest to the velocity actually used in training will be most affected. Studies also indicate that the greatest gains in strength will be made at the velocity at which training was performed. Thus, if it is necessary to be strong at a fast velocity to be successful in a particular sport, training at a fast velocity using proper barbell exercises (such as pulls, cleans or with proper equipment, such as isokinetics or hydraulic or pneumatic) at some point during the training cycle would be advantageous, if not essential. This does not mean that all training should be done at a fast velocity—only that some weight training at some point in the training cycle needs to be done this way. For the athlete, the point in a training cycle where fast velocity or power training is normally performed is in the pre-season, late pre-season, and prior to major competitions.

Muscle Action Specificity. Two major types of muscle action can be performed on commonly available resistance training equipment. Dynamic muscle actions occur when movement actually takes place. Isometric actions occur when no movement takes place at a joint.

Dynamic muscle actions are what most people consider to be normal weight training. From the starting position of most weight training exercises, when the muscle shortens the weight is lifted. This is termed a concentric (or positive) muscle action. From the top, or finish, position of most exercises the weight must then be returned to the starting position. When the weight is returned to the starting position, the same muscles that lifted it are activated and go through a controlled lengthening process. This is termed an eccentric (or negative) muscle action (Figure 2.3). If the muscles that lifted the weight did not perform this controlled eccentric muscle action, the weight would simply drop back to the starting position for lack of a counter force to oppose gravity.

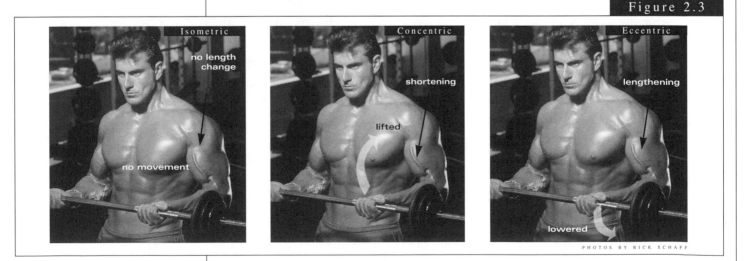

Figure 2.3

PHOTOS BY RICK SCHAFF

Figure 2.3. *Isometric, concentric and eccentric: three types of muscle actions.*

An isometric muscle action can be performed by pushing against an immovable object, such as a wall or a weight machine, or even a barbell loaded beyond what the individual can actually lift with a concentric action. Isometric muscle actions are important in many sports. During wrestling and judo, isometric actions are constantly being performed as the athletes push and pull each other in the fight for position.

In sporting events, concentric muscle actions are necessary to produce the power that results in movement of the athlete's body, or the movement of objects such as a ball. Eccentric muscle actions are necessary to decelerate or slow down the athlete's body. After an object like a ball is released, eccentric muscle actions slow down the arm and the rest of the body. If the arm is not slowed down in a controlled manner, injury can result. Concentric/eccentric muscle actions are vital for both sporting and daily life activities.

Since normal weight training utilizes both eccentric and concentric muscle actions, it results in both eccentric and concentric strength gains and often an increase in muscle size. To optimally enhance performance in some sports the use of heavy eccentric resistances may not be necessary, or even desirable. However, there are some sports where the use of heavy negatives may be quite advantageous. As a cogent example, one factor that separates very elite powerlifters from good powerlifters is the ability to slowly lower the weight during the squat and bench press lifts. Performance of heavy negatives at a slow velocity may be key in the training of a powerlifter.

VARIATION PRINCIPLE

Variety in the training program—touched upon in chapter 1—is a periodization cornerstone. Encouragingly, there are many different ways to get variety into your program. These include light, moderate, and heavy days in the course of a week; or light, moderate, and heavy weeks of training during the course of a month. Changes in the exercises are an excellent way to add variety. You'd be surprised how easily you can freshen your routine by substituting a dumbbell bench press, or a machine chest press for a barbell bench press. Further, changes in hand or foot spacing during arm or leg exercises can be used to add variety to a training program. When you consider it, virtually anything that can be changed in a training program can be changed to add variety. The purpose, of course, of adding variety to a program is to change the training stimulus and provide recovery so that the muscles and body continue to adapt—resulting, as noted, in optimal gains in strength, power, muscle size, and athletic performance.

Variety in training is one of the keys to continued gains and the key to avoiding long-term training plateaus. Just make sure you're not one of those individuals who has a retentive mania for sameness and routine both in your training regimen and your daily life!

DETRAINING PRINCIPLE

In general, whenever training is stopped, any gains will begin to erode. Figure 2.4 depicts changes in maximal strength during a two-week detraining period in male strength athletes, physically active males, and physically active females after ten-and-a-half weeks of training. Both the physically active females and male strength athletes showed small decreases in maximal strength during the two week detraining period. Interestingly, the physically active males showed a small increase in maximal strength during the two-week detraining period. This indicates that not all people will show a decrease in maximal strength during short detraining periods.

Whether a decrease in strength or a small increase in strength occurs during a short detraining period is probably dependent upon the training that immediately proceeded this period. If training was very stressful immediately prior to the short detraining period, a gain in strength may be apparent because the individual will simply be recovering from the intense training. However, during longer detraining periods (e.g., several weeks or months), physical abilities will dramatically decrease.

This concept—that a short detraining period, if preceded by a very intense training period, will result in little or no loss or possibly even a gain in strength—can be used to a trainee's advantage in some situations. In fact, it is the basis of many periodized program strategies. For example, during a one or two-week vacation period, erosion of strength and muscle size can be minimized by engaging in a very intense training period right before the vacation. Ideally, the vacation then acts as a useful recovery time.

The same principle can be used in the planning of any periodized training program. Such a time period might be right before a major competition for some athletes and in-season for other athletes, depending on the nature of the sport or event. In almost Zen-like fashion, we can see how not-doing becomes a form of doing. Be careful, though! If no weight training is performed for too long a period, eventually a significant decrease in strength, power, and muscle size will occur.

Knowledge of detraining is also important when it comes to minimizing physical losses during a period of reduced training. A period of reduced training should be preceded by a relatively intense period of training. Even during the period of reduced training, one to two weight training sessions per week should be performed. If the weight training sessions are performed at the same intensity as the sessions that preceded the reduced training period, strength can be maintained for up to a period of at least eight weeks. Thus, even during the competition phase of a yearly training plan, some resistance training should be performed to prevent or slow the loss of gains in strength, power and muscle size made during the off-season and pre-season training program.

INDIVIDUALIZATION PRINCIPLE

For any training program to result in optimal gains, it must address an individual's strengths, weaknesses and previous injuries, as well as their goals and needs. All principles must therefore come under the umbrella of the individualization principle. In the case of prior injuries, exercises that strengthen muscle groups in common injury sites or trouble areas need to be included. In general, the most common site of injury in many sports is the knee. Accordingly, exercises that strengthen the quadriceps and hamstring muscle groups should tend to be included in your regimen.

These general training principles provide guidance for the design of all resistance training programs. The next chapter goes into some depth into actual changes within a program. Remember, your periodization regimen will be most effective if you start with a firm understanding of general principles—and how the individualization principle applies to you—and then get into the nuts-and-bolts specifics of your ongoing regimen.

Figure 2.4

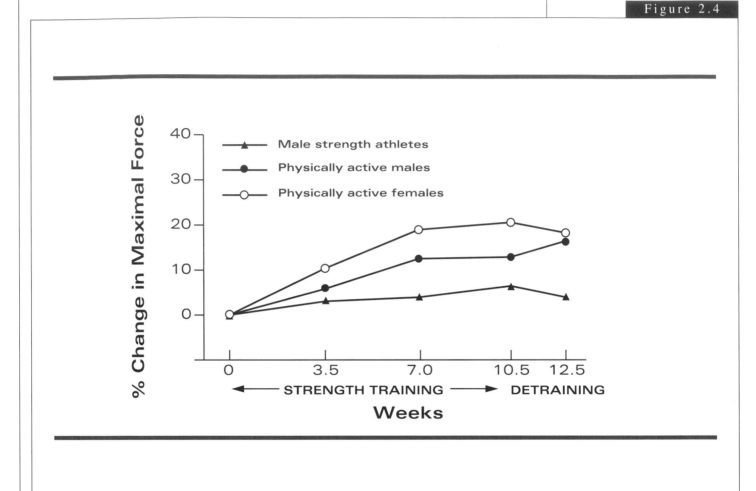

Figure 2.4. *Effect on maximal strength of a two-week detraining period on three different groups. Data from Häkkinen K., Pakarinen, A., Komi, P., Ryushi, T., and Kauhanen, H. Neuromuscular adaptations and hormone balance in strength athletes, physically active males and females during intensive strength training. Proceedings of the XII International Congress of Biomechanics in Education. Gregor, R.J., Zernicke, R.F., Whiting, W.C., 1989.*

SELECTED READINGS:

- *Fleck, S.J. and Kraemer, W.J. (1988). Resistance training: basic principles (part 1 of 4). The Physician and Sports Medicine, 16:160-171.*
- *Kraemer, W.J., Deschenes, M.R., and Fleck, S.J. (1988). Physiological adaptations to resistance exercise implications for athletic conditioning. Sports Medicine, 6:246-256.*
- *Häkkinen, K., Pakarinen, A., Komi, P., Ryushi, T., and Kauhanen, H. Neuromuscular adaptations and hormone balance in strength athletes, physically active males and females during intensive strength training. In: Proceedings of the XII International Congress of Biomechanics, (ed.) Gregor, R.J., Zernicke, R.F., Whiting, R.C., 1989.*

what can be changed?

Virtually anything in a workout that can be changed can be manipulated in a periodized training program. The key is to make logical changes that will help meet the goals of the program. Possible variables in a weight training program are listed in the following Table.

TABLE 3.1.
THINGS THAT CAN BE CHANGED IN A TRAINING PROGRAM

- number of repetitions per set
- weight or resistance used
- number of sets per exercise
- exercises performed
- exercise order
- rest periods between sets and exercises
- rest periods between training sessions

NUMBER OF REPETITIONS PER SET

Changing the number of repetitions per set is probably the most common of the training variables. In general, the guidelines for the number of repetitions per set are described in terms of training zones. In very general terms, if the major goal of training is to increase maximal strength/power, then one to six repetitions per set are performed. If the major goal of training is to increase muscular size, then in general a range of six to 12 repetitions per set are performed. When the major goal of training is to increase local muscular endurance and cardiovascular endurance, then 13 to 20 repetitions per set are performed.

In general, for the above guidelines to be true the resistance used for a specified number of repetitions per set must be performed at or close to a repetition maximum (RM) resistance (see chapter 2, the Overload Principle section, for the definition of RM). As with all types of exercise training, if the effort is too easy the body will not make adaptations. Although we went into this somewhat in chapter 2, here's another example: if you are physically capable of running three miles in 24 minutes, and you insist on running three miles in 34 minutes during training, you will make little or no gain in cardiovascular endurance or your performance time. As is evident, the training is too easy for your cardiovascular system's fitness level.

The same is true for weight training. If the weight used is too light, the training stimulus is insufficient to promote strength gains. The use of a resistance close to the RM ensures that the training stimulus is sufficient to bring about an increase in a specific fitness variable (e.g., muscular size, strength/power, local muscular and cardiovascular endurance). This does not mean that a RM weight must be used for all sets of

Figure 3.1

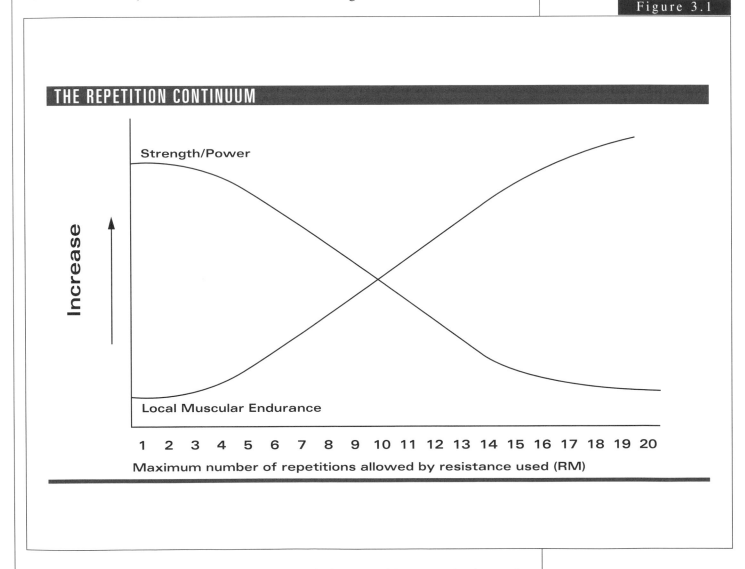

Figure 3.1. *The repetition continuum demonstrates whether strength/power or local muscular endurance is being emphasized when doing a certain number of repetitions per set.*

an exercise, but that close to a RM resistance must be used for at least some part of the training program.

The guidelines for the number of repetitions per set are not pure cut-off points, related to major training goals. Rather, the number of repetitions per set functions on a continuum. For example, five repetitions per set does not train all maximal strength/power and seven repetitions per set all muscular size. Rather, a 5 RM weight used to perform five repetitions per set trains mostly maximal strength/power; some muscular size; and very little local muscular or cardiovascular endurance. While a 7 RM weight used to perform seven repetitions per set is training slightly less for maximal strength/power; slightly more for muscular size; and slightly more for local and cardiovascular endurance than five repetitions per set. There is a gradual switch over from one training outcome to another as the number of repetitions per set is increased or decreased (Figure 3.1). Complex? Yes, but nothing you can't get a handle on.

WEIGHT OR RESISTANCE USED

The weight or resistance used during a set in part determines how many repetitions can be performed (bet you knew that). It follows that it is impossible to perform a large number of repetitions in a set if the chosen weight is near the 1 RM.

Ideally, a resistance of at least 60% of the 1 RM needs to be used if strength is going to be optimally developed. Many strength/conditioning coaches do not, in fact, count a set as part of the actual training session if less resistance is employed. Anything less than 60% of the 1 RM is counted as a mere warm-up set.

If proper exercise technique for a new exercise is being emphasized—as indeed it should be—then a light resistance needs to be used. Normally, a resistance that allows at least 10 repetitions per set should be employed when learning proper exercise technique. A lighter resistance also should be used if an experienced lifter is attempting to correct a flaw in exercise technique.

It is not necessary to keep the same weight or number of repetitions per set for all sets of an exercise performed in the same training session. Thus, it is possible to develop many different patterns in number of repetitions and weight used. Some popular combinations include a pyramid; an ascending half-pyramid; and a descending half-pyramid. A pyramid is a pattern of decreasing number of repetitions per set with increasing weight; followed by increasing number of reps per set with a decrease in weight (Figure 3.2). An ascending half-pyramid consists of performing only the first half, or decreasing number, of repetitions per set part of a pyramid. A descending half-pyramid consists of performing, after an essential warm-up, only the second half, or increasing repetitions, per set part of a pyramid.

There is no real consensus concerning which pattern of number of repetitions per set and weight used is best. (In fact, there is considerable room for debate within the realm of exercise science.) The individual designing the program must rely on the basic guidelines concerning weight used and number of repetitions for expected outcomes. In fact, the variation principle (see chapter 2) indicates that the use of several set and repetition schemes may be needed at different times in training to bring about optimal fitness gains.

Figure 3.2

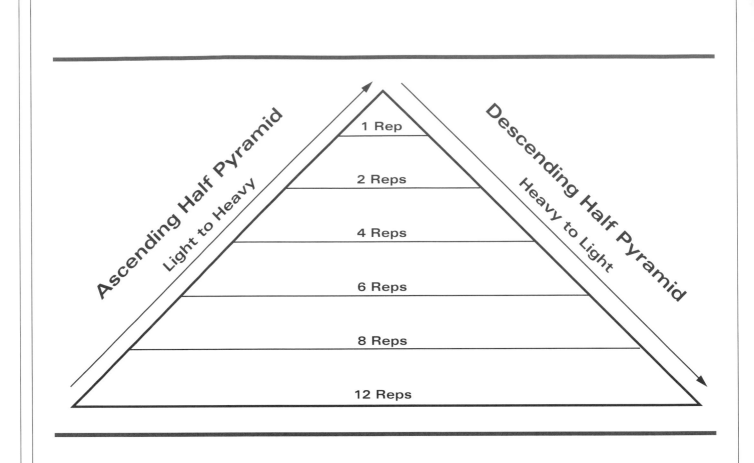

Figure 3.2. A pyramid consists of performing a decreasing number of repetitions per set while increasing the weight used, followed by an increase in the number of repetitions per set with a decrease in the weight used. An ascending half-pyramid consists of doing only the first part (or decreasing number) of repetitions per set portion of a pyramid. While a descending half-pyramid consists of doing only the second part (or increasing number) of repetitions per set portion of a pyramid.

NUMBER OF SETS

Increases in strength/power and muscle size do occur when one set of an exercise per training session is performed by previously untrained people (American College of Sports Medicine, 1990). However, the majority of evidence supports the idea that multiple sets of an exercise result in greater gains in strength/power and muscle size than just one set. Three sets of an exercise seems to be the minimal number needed to bring about near-maximal gains in strength/power and muscular size. Many athletes, however, perform more than three sets of an exercise per training session. In general, six sets is the maximal number.

One set programs can be useful in various instances that don't involve rank beginners. One set can be useful to individuals who have a very limited amount of training time but still desire to do some weight training. These individuals are oftentimes business professionals interested in general fitness who desire to get into better physical condition, maintain their present physical condition, feel better, or improve body composition. In other words, their goals are severely proscribed, or even modest. Whether these individuals attain a certain goal this month or next month (or never) is not really critical—at least to their mind. Nevertheless, individuals who desire higher levels of fitness will need, at some point, to advance to more sophisticated multiple-set programs. There's just no way of getting around that, infomercial "miracle devices" or no.

One-set programs can also be used in-season by athletes who in the off-season utilize a multiple-set program. This is done in an attempt to slow the loss of strength/power and muscular size during the season, when only a limited amount of time is available to perform weight training. This type of in-season program does slow—but indeed may not completely stop—the diminution of strength/power.

Even if only one set of an exercise is performed per training session, it does not mean other training variables cannot be altered to add variety to an in-season program. The exercise choice, exercise order, number of repetitions per set, rest periods between exercises and other training variables can and should be manipulated in the name of an effective periodized regimen.

It's important to note again that it is not necessary that each exercise be performed for the same number of sets in a session. Let's take a specific example. Say it is your desire to stress upper thigh development. While the majority of exercises may be limited to three sets, you might choose to do five sets of squats, knee extensions and leg curls, putting the emphasis on specific muscle groups in order to meet your training goals for that particular period.

Now you're beginning to understand why periodization is such an effective training method!

E X E R C I S E   C H O I C E

The muscle groups you need to train dictate the type of exercise movements. If you're looking to train the elbow flexors (biceps and some of the wrist flexors), you're going to be doing some arm curls. If you're looking to concentrate on the front of the thigh (quadriceps group), knee extensions will figure into your regimen.

An athlete, as indicated, will chose exercises based on the physical demands and injury specificity of his/her sport. If the program is geared towards the hardcore bodybuilder, exercises that will develop total body hypertrophy and definition need to be the focus. The bodybuilder will also look for exercises that will develop specific muscle groups that are the weak point of their physique, or of major importance in the posing routine (depending perhaps on the perceived inclination of the judges). For a lady or gentleman interested in general fitness, at least one exercise for all the major muscle groups needs to be included.

One choice that needs to be made is whether to use a machine or free weights. For some exercises the choice is easy, because they can only be performed with either one

Figure 3.3

PHOTO BY PER BERNAL

Figure 3.3. *When performing an exercise with a barbell or dumbbell, the weight must be balanced and motion controlled in several directions: up and down; forward and backward; and left to right.*

or the other. For example, knee extensions and knee curls are typically performed only on machines; while an exercise like a power clean is only performed using free weights.

Some strength and conditioning coaches believe that free weight exercises more closely resemble everyday and athletic activities (Figure 3.3). The weight must be balanced in forward, backward and side-to-side planes of movement, and lifted and lowered accordingly. Therefore, many strength coaches prefer athletes to use free weights.

Because of the need to balance the weight in all three planes of movement, some exercise techniques for free weight exercises take longer to learn than the proper technique for machine exercises. This is because the weight resistance is traditionally only lifted and lowered, as most machines do not allow any side-to-side or forward and backward movement. Many see this as an advantage of machines. The bottom line is that both free weights and machines can be effective tools in a weight training program if matched properly to the needs and goals of the trainee.

Another common area of choice is whether to perform multi-joint or a single-joint exercises. Multi-joint exercises, as the name indicates, require movement at more than one joint, and train more than one muscle group. Exercises like back squats, deadlifts and power cleans are multi-joint exercises (Figure 3.4). Single-joint exercises allow movement only at one joint and predominantly train only one muscle or muscle group. Exercises like arm curls, triceps extensions and calf raises are single-joint exercises.

One advantage of multi-joint exercises is that the lifter learns to coordinate different muscles so they work as a unit. This is important in many activities and sports which require multi-joint muscle coordination. Another advantage of multi-joint exer-

Figure 3.4

PHOTO BY MITSURU OKABE

Figure 3.4. When performing structural or multi-joint exercises, like the back squat, movement takes place at several joints and several muscle groups are active. When performing a single joint exercise, like knee extensions, movement takes place at predominantly one joint and only one muscle group is active.

cises is they do train more than one muscle, so it takes fewer exercises to train all the major muscle groups of the body. This allows a training session to be made up of fewer exercises and therefore take less time to perform. But keep in mind that the amount of weight lifted and the number of repetitions performed with a given weight is limited by the weakest muscle or muscle group utilized during a multi-joint exercise. Thus, not all muscles used in a multi-joint exercise may be receiving an optimal training stimulus. Similar to free weight exercises in general, it takes longer to learn proper technique for most multi-joint exercises. (See Figure 3.4 on previous page.)

The main advantage of single-joint exercises is the ability to isolate and therefore train a particular muscle or muscle group. This can be especially useful to the bodybuilder who wants to emphasize a particular muscle. Also, the need to isolate a muscle or muscle group is all-important in rehabilitation settings; and is, of course, an effective way to train a muscle or muscle group that is prone to injury.

Bottom line: due to advantages and disadvantages of free weight versus machine exercises and single versus multi-joint exercises, most training programs will have a combination of approaches. A prime goal in the choice of exercises is to exploit the advantages and minimize the weaknesses of each and every possibility.

EXERCISE ORDER

Exercise order can have an impact on both how the lifter feels during the session and on the training stimulus provided by said session. There are many typical exercise orders. Alternating from one muscle group to another muscle group—such as elbow curls (arms) followed by knee extensions (legs)—is popular. The opposite side of the coin is to "stack" or perform exercises for the same muscle group or body part in succession: such as elbow pushdowns followed by dumbbell kick-backs. This type of order does not allow recovery between exercises for a muscle group and it is more stressful than alternating muscle groups. So exercise order affects how much recovery time is allowed between exercises for the same muscle group, which is an important consideration.

If power type exercises are included, they are many times performed early in the training session. This ensures they will be completed before the lifter has been too taxed. The goal of this type exercise—such as variations on Olympic lifts (snatch, clean and jerk) and plyometrics—is to improve maximal power. If the lifter is fatigued prior to performing them, the power goal will remain elusive, to say the least. This same line of reasoning applies to exercises that focus on maximal strength development using 1-3 RM resistances (e.g., the squat and bench press). Do 'em early on in the session, or suffer the consequences.

Another common exercise order is known as the priority system. Those exercises with the highest priority in terms of fitness goals are performed early in the session, followed by exercises of descending priority. If your major goal is to strengthen legs, you know you'll be hitting them early on.

As with all of the training variables, exercise order needs to be quite seriously considered. Never let this decision be random, or due to a superficial reason like how the equipment is arranged in the gym.

REST PERIODS BETWEEN SETS AND EXERCISES

The length of rest periods between sets and exercises should be chosen to meet training goals. It should never be based on how long it takes to chat with a friend or get a drink of water from the fountain on the other side of the gym. The length of the rest period should be based only on the desired outcome of the training.

Rest periods can be divided into short—less than a minute; medium—one to three minutes; and long—greater than three minutes. Short rest periods are normally used when you desire to train for local muscular endurance, because short rests result in high blood lactate concentrations. Lactate is a by-product of anaerobic metabolism that builds up in the blood during long periods of intense exercise, or short periods of intense exercise separated by short rest periods. Lactate is in part the cause of muscular fatigue and the needles-and-pins feeling following a strenuous activity like running 400 meters as fast as possible; or performing six sets of 10 RM squats with one-minute rest periods between sets. Over the course of time, weight training with short rest periods does cause the body to become accustomed to higher blood lactate levels and to remove lactate from the blood faster, thus improving local muscular endurance.

The effect of rest period length between sets (and exercises) on blood lactate concentration in men when using a 10 RM resistance is depicted in Figure 3.5. Three sets

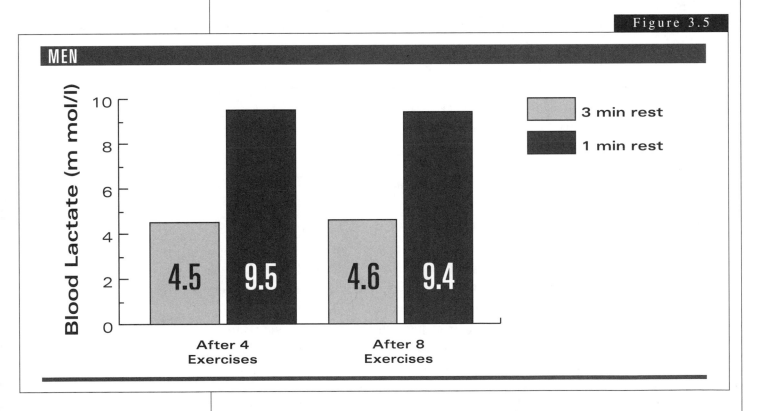

Figure 3.5 *Blood lactate concentrations of men during workouts of three sets of eight exercises at a 10 RM resistance with either a one- or three-minute rest period between sets and exercises. Data from W.J. Kraemer et al., 1990, "Hormonal and growth factor responses to heavy resistance exercise protocols." Journal of Applied Physiology, 69, p. 1445.*

Figure 3.6

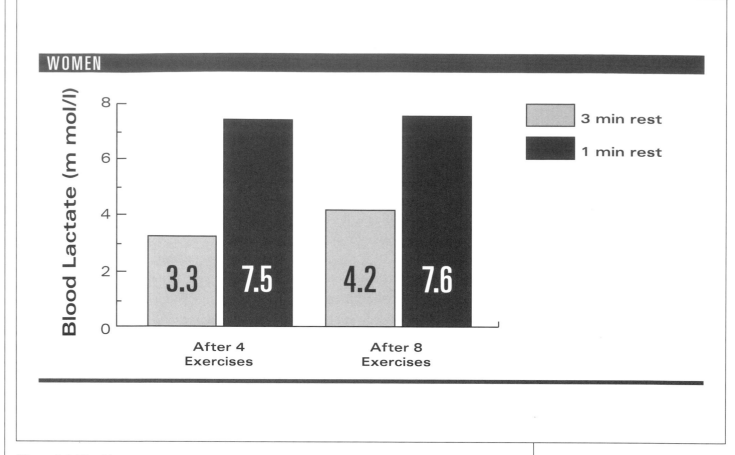

WOMEN

Figure 3.6. Blood lactate concentrations of women during workouts of three sets of eight exercises at a 10 RM resistance with either a one- or three-minute rest period between sets and exercises. Data from W.J. Kraemer et al., 1990, "Hormonal and growth factor responses to heavy resistance exercise protocols". Journal of Applied Physiology, 69, pp. 1442-1450.

at a 10 RM resistance of the same variety of eight exercises were performed during two different workouts. The only difference between the workouts was that in one a one-minute rest period was allowed, and in the other there was a three-minute rest period. Blood lactate concentration during and after the workout with one-minute rest periods was twice as great as in the one with three-minute rest periods. A similar blood lactate response occurred in women with parallel changes in rest periods (Figure 3.6). Without doubt, the length of rest periods can have a very dramatic effect on blood lactate concentrations, and therefore the perceived stress of the workout.

Extremely short rest periods of 30 seconds or less are used during circuit weight training programs where an increase in cardiovascular fitness is desired. The short rest periods contribute to a higher heart rate for a longer period of time than occurs with normal "heavy" weight training. This helps to increase cardiovascular fitness. Extremely short rest periods, as noted, quickly result in high blood lactate concentrations and produce enough fatigue so that a weight heavy enough to result in large gains in strength becomes impossible to use.

A circuit weight training program for untrained people causes a five to eight percent cardiovascular fitness increase over 15 to 20 weeks of training (Gettman and Pollock, 1981). A running, swimming or cycling training program causes a 15-25% cardiovascular fitness increase in untrained people over the same time period. So, if the major goal of a program is to increase cardiovascular fitness, weight training may not be the best choice for most individuals.

Medium-length rest periods are employed when the desire is to cause an increase in muscle size. Rest periods of this length result in a blood hormonal profile—increased growth hormone and testosterone—that lends itself to muscle growth (Kraemer et al., 1990; Kraemer et al., 1991; Kraemer et al., 1993). A medium-length rest period also allows enough recovery between sets to allow the use a heavy enough weight so an increase in strength/power occurs.

Long rest periods of three minutes or greater are most appropriate when the major goal is to increase maximal strength/power. This will allow sufficient recovery between sets and exercises so that near-maximal resistances for the desired number of repetitions can be used. We'll emphasize this point numerous times throughout the chapters.

REST PERIODS BETWEEN TRAINING SESSIONS

Many trainees undertake three weight training sessions per week with at least one day of rest between sessions. Such a pattern would typically be to train on Mondays, Wednesdays, and Fridays, allowing for an ample recovery period on off-days and weekends.

Were a strength test to be given prior to a session and immediately after a session, it would appear that there was actually a decrease in the trainee's strength. This apparent decrease is due to fatigue. In reality the training session provides the stimulus for the body to make adaptations, such as an increase in muscle size. But, as we cannot emphasize enough, it is between training sessions that adaptations are made. For most people, a 24-hour period seems sufficient for the body to recover and make some adaptations to training. Thus, for the individual interested in general fitness, three training sessions per week appears to be a sufficient stimulus to make gains.

But, for better or for worse, nothing is ever quite that simple. In reality, the three-days-per-week guideline is true for individual muscle groups and not the whole body. What it is essentially saying is that training of a certain muscle group can occur every other day with a day of rest between sessions. Concentrating on a variety of muscle groups—while always allowing for sufficient rest for each specific group—has led to the development of programs where training may take place six or even seven days per week, without overly taxing a certain muscle group. Therefore, many training patterns can and have been developed that go beyond the three-days-a-week recommendation.

A four-days-on/one-day-off training schedule is shown in Table 3.2. In this training pattern the four days of training and one day of rest are performed in succession on whatever day of the week they happen to occur. In the training sessions outlined each muscle group is trained every five days.

T A B L E 3 . 2 .
F O U R - O N / O N E - O F F S C H E D U L E

Day 1 : hamstrings, shoulders
Day 2 : back, biceps, abdominals
Day 3 : front of thighs, calves
Day 4 : chest, triceps
Day 5 : off

Another possible training schedule is six-on/one-off and this is outlined in Table 3.3. With this type of training schedule each muscle group is trained two times every seven days. It is not necessary—or even the ideal situation—when working out on a six-on/one-off training schedule to use exactly the same exercises when training a given muscle group on two successive occasions within the same seven-day period. Here's a schedule that opens the door to a healthy variety of exercise choice, while still allowing for sufficient muscle group recovery time.

T A B L E 3 . 3 .
S I X - O N / O N E - O F F S C H E D U L E

Day 1 : shoulders, arms, abdominals
Day 2 : thighs, legs
Day 3 : back, chest
Day 4 : same as day 1
Day 5 : same as day 2
Day 6 : same as day 3
Day 7 : off

Stay with us on this one now, because we're going to shake things up a little more. Some programs do have trainees exercising the same body part or performing the same exercise on successive days, even to the point of extreme excess. But what about the recovery period? One Eastern European program for Olympic style weightlifters using multiple training sessions on the same day supposedly had the athletes squatting 16 times a week. Not much room for recovery there, you say. Well, several things must be considered when examining such programs. These type programs are normally only performed for short periods of time, not all year around. These are very advanced programs only for elite athletes and are clearly not recommended for recreational lifters or people lifting for general fitness. But it does show you that the rules can be broken, and sometimes to considerably positive effect.

Let's stay on this a bit longer: a practice becoming more prevalent among elite athletes is to perform more than one training session on the same day. Initially, this may have begun as an attempt to increase total training volume. Depending upon the athlete's condition and the program being performed, some increase in the training volume may perhaps be beneficial. However, more is not always better—or, to put it another way, less is more—and the volume can be increased to a point where the program cannot be adapted to or even tolerated, due to woefully insufficient recovery ability between training sessions. This will result in overuse injuries and an actual decrease in fitness.

There is, however, evidence that performing two training sessions on the same day with no increase in total training volume is beneficial to elite athletes. In fact, taking a normal training session and cutting it in half—i.e., performing half in the morning and half in the afternoon—can lead to greater gains in strength than performing all the training during one session (Häkkinen and Pakarinen, 1991). This is probably due to the fact that splitting the session tends to keep training intensity as high as possible. Key to this is that the total training volume must be carefully monitored and controlled; otherwise the purpose of the whole approach is defeated.

So, yes, five or six training days per week can be tolerated if properly planned and periodized. Let's even go so far as to say that multiple training sessions on the same day can also be tolerated if properly planned. But a cardinal rule still applies: time must be allowed for the body to recover and adapt to the increased training load.

The "rule of soreness" is a good means of judging whether or not the trainee is adapting to the increased load. If the trainee is severely sore at the start of the follow-up training session, or cannot complete a training session that had been completed previously, it is time to consider if the total training load is too great. Maybe even well past time! Don't get carried away!

Remember, all of the training variables discussed in this chapter need to be considered when designing a program. All the variables interact with each other—to ignore one is to fatally upset the balance of the others. Likewise, changes in training variables must be carefully considered and controlled, or the body's adaptations will be made haphazardly, to the detriment of your fitness progress and goals. This will result in less than an optimal training program, which flys in the face of what periodization is all about. Think of all those variables and individual changes within variables as being like stones tossed into a lake: every one of those stones will cause a ripple effect. And where those ripples stop—and how they intersect—can be a tricky business to determine. So make sure you know what you're doing, and then carry on.

In the next chapter, we'll delve into the terminology of periodization—if you plan to get with the program, you have to know the lingo!

SELECTED READINGS:
• *American College of Sports Medicine (1990). The recommended quantity and quality of exercise for developing and maintaining cardiovascular and muscular fitness in healthy adults. Medicine and Science in Sports and Exercise, 22, 265-274.*
• *Gettman, L.R. and Pollock, M.J. (1981). Circuit weight training: A critical review of its physiological benefits. The Physician and Sports Medicine, 9, 44-60.*
• *Häkkinen, K. and Pakarinen, A. (1991). Serum hormones in male strength athletes during intense short-term strength training. European Journal of Applied Physiology, 63, 194-199.*
• *Kraemer, W.J., Fleck, S.J., Dziados, J.E., Harman, E.A., Marchitelli, L.J., Gordon, S.E., Mello, R., Frykman, P.N., Koziris, L.P. and Triplett, N.T. (1993). Changes in*

hormonal concentrations after different heavy-resistance exercise protocols in women. Journal of Applied Physiology, 75, 594-604.

- *Kraemer, W.J., Gordon, S.E., Fleck, S.J., Marchitelli, L.J., Mello, R., Dziados, J.E., Friedl, K., Harman, E., Maresh, C. and Fry, A.C. (1991). Endogenous anabolic hormonal and growth factor responses to heavy resistance exercise in males and females. International Journal of Sports Medicine, 12, 228-235.*

- *Kraemer, W.J., Marchitelli, L.J., McCurry, D., Mello, R., Dziados, J.E., Harman, E., Frykman, P., Gordon, S.E. and Fleck, S.J. (1990). Hormonal and growth factor responses to heavy resistance exercise. Journal of Applied Physiology, 69, 1442-1450.*

periodization terminology

esoteric terminology can make it difficult to understand a periodization program. However, all periodization terminology either describes a certain type of training; a certain portion of a training year; or a certain length of time within a training year.

Europeans are normally credited with developing the original terminology. Some Americans still rely on this European terminology. However, others have developed an Americanized terminology unique unto itself. But as long as you're clear what you're talking about, it all comes down to the "rose by any other name" principle.

Thus, there are at least three variations:

1. indigenous American terminology;
2. traditional European terminology; and
3. American terminology that grew out of traditional European terminology.

Before any type of periodization terminology can be discussed, the terms "training volume" and "intensity" need to be defined. Volume refers to the total amount of training. In a running or cycling program, volume is defined as the total miles ran or cycled. In weight training, volume is defined as the total number of repetitions performed in a time period (such as a week or month). Weight training volume can also be defined as the total amount of weight lifted. In this case, volume is determined by multiplying the number of repetitions by the weight lifted. As an example, if 10 repetitions are performed using 100 pounds, the volume is 1000 pounds (10 repetitions x 100 pounds).

Training intensity refers to the difficulty of the training. In running or cycling, intensity can be defined by the percentage of maximal heart rate at which the training was performed; or, by the time it takes to run or cycle a certain distance. Intensity of weight training can be defined as the average weight lifted. However, in most cases it is easier to understand weight training intensity if it is described as a percentage of the maximal possible weight that can be lifted for one repetition (1 RM) or any other number of repetitions. As an example, performing 10 repetitions at 100% of the maximal weight possible (10 RM) would be as intense as training with 10 repetitions can get. Doing ten repetitions with 90% of the maximal 10 RM weight possible would be less intense, if minimally so.

TRADITIONAL AMERICAN TERMINOLOGY

Most Americans think of a sports competition year as being made up of three major phases. These phases are the off-season, pre-season, and in-season.

Off-Season. The off-season begins after the last competition of a season and ends when training for the next season begins. The length of the off-season is, in part, determined by the length of the season for a particular sport. For sports with a very long in-season, such as professional basketball and baseball, the off-season is relatively short. Whereas the season for a softball league might run six weeks, so we'd be talking about a really lengthy off-season.

The term off-season implies—at least to the uninitiated—that no training is being performed. However, if that were the case, physical conditioning and sport specific skills would quickly deteriorate. Therefore, it is important to perform some moderate intensity and moderate-to-low volume training in the off-season. If physical conditioning and sport skills are allowed to deteriorate dramatically, it will be difficult to enter the next season in anything resembling competitive shape, let alone in better physical condition than the season just completed.

Attempting to "play" yourself into shape during the season only means you are not in good condition at the start of the season. Performance—at least initially—will be less than optimal. Many a season has been lost for this reason, no matter how valiant an attempt the team makes to catch up in the home stretch. In addition, attempting to play yourself into shape can (and probably will) result in injury. Getting in shape after the season starts is obviously not a viable alternative.

Pre-Season. The pre-season begins when serious training in preparation for the next season starts, and ends when the first competition of the season takes place. It is a period of time when sport-specific training is undertaken. Similar to the off-season, the length of the pre-season is, in part, determined by the actual season's length.

It is difficult to get into good enough condition to play a given sport in a period of less than two to three months. Therefore, pre-season for any sport should be at least that long. The pre-season normally starts with high-volume and low-intensity physical conditioning and skill work for the sport.

As the season approaches, the intensity of physical conditioning increases and the volume of physical conditioning decreases (Figure 4.1). The volume of skill training for a sport or activity increases as the season approaches. The goal of the pre-season is to get into the best possible physical condition and optimally develop the skills needed to be successful in a particular sport.

In-Season. The in-season begins with the first competition of the year and ends with the last competition of the year. Normally, the volume of physical training is low and the intensity of physical training high during the in-season. Skill training for the sport during the in-season is also normally high. The goal during in-season is to maintain physical conditioning and skill levels for the entire season and to achieve peak skill levels and physical conditioning for the major competitions normally found at the end of the season, such as conference, regional, state, and national championships.

Figure 4.1

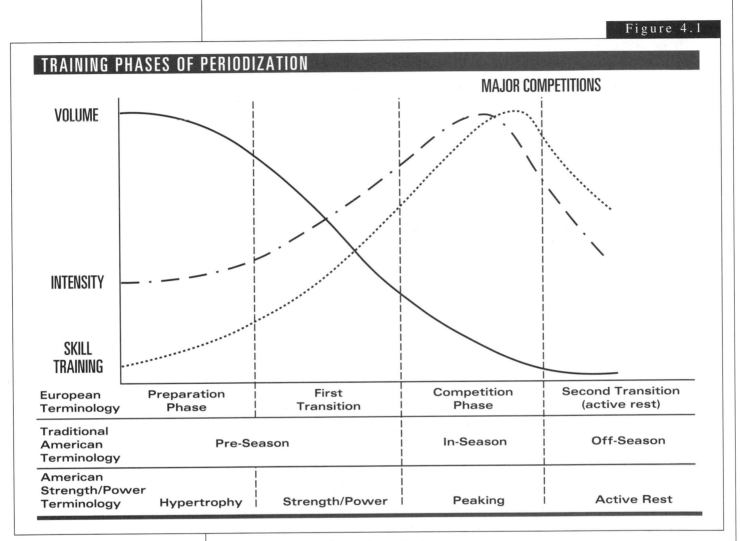

TRAINING PHASES OF PERIODIZATION

European Terminology	Preparation Phase	First Transition	Competition Phase	Second Transition (active rest)
Traditional American Terminology	Pre-Season		In-Season	Off-Season
American Strength/Power Terminology	Hypertrophy	Strength/Power	Peaking	Active Rest

Figure 4.1. *Training phases of periodization.*

TRADITIONAL EUROPEAN TERMINOLOGY

Traditional European terminology consists of three general types. The first describes the phase length of a particular training period. The second type is similar to America's off-season, pre-season, and in-season, describing where, within the training year, each phase occurs. The third area of terminology describes a particular type of training.

THE TRAINING PHASE LENGTH

All terms under this heading describe the length of a particular training phase, with different terms to describe a week, a month, and a year of training.

Macrocycle. Normally used to describe one entire training year. A macrocycle is generally thought of as beginning and ending after the last competition of a season. Macrocycle is also sometimes used to describe a length of time longer than one year. As an example, it is used to describe the time between such major competitions as the Winter or Summer Olympics—that is, a four-year time period.

Mesocycle. This term was originally used to describe the major training phases of an entire training year. The preparation, first transition, competition and second transition phases were described as mesocycles (Figure 4.1). Thus, mesocycle originally referred to a time period of two to three months. However, with the advent of the idea that to ensure optimal gains in physical conditioning, changes in training should be made every four to six weeks, this term has been altered to mean a training period lasting that length of time. Throughout this chapter, mesocycle will be used in this shorter context.

Microcycle. Microcycle refers to one week or seven days of training. If three training sessions per week are performed, microcycle refers to those three sessions. If six training sessions per week are performed, then microcycle refers to six sessions. However, no matter how many training sessions are performed per week, microcycle always refers to seven days or one week of training.

TRAINING PHASE LOCATION

In this case, training phases refer to particular time periods within a total training year. These training phases tend to refer to such similar time periods within the year as the American off-season, pre-season, and in-season. Each training phase is made up of several mesocycles.

Preparation Phase. This phase parallels the early pre-season in traditional American terminology. The major goal of this training phase is to develop basic physical conditioning in preparation for the upcoming season or competitions. Training within this phase is normally of a relatively high-volume and relatively low-intensity.

First Transition. Refers to the late pre-season in traditional American terminology. Compared to the preparation phase, the intensity of training is higher and the volume of training is lower. The goal of this training phase is to make the transition from the preparation phase to the competition or in-season training phase.

Competition Phase. This phase is analogous to the in-season. The competition phase normally ends with a major event such as a conference or state championship. During the competition phase, the training intensity normally reaches its maximum and the training volume its minimum for the year. The goal of this phase is to maintain physical condition and sport specific skills for the entire season, and to peak the athlete for major competitions.

Second Transition. The equivalent of the American off-season. It is also sometimes referred to as the active rest phase. The goal of this training phase is to allow the individual to recover both psychologically and physically from the in-season or competition phase. "Active rest" accurately describes what should take place during this phase: the athlete rests and recovers from the in-season or competition phase. However, some exercise training should be performed so that the trainee's physical condition does not deteriorate drastically. The activity may be in the form of exercise not typically performed in training.

TYPES OF TRAINING

The following terms refer to broad types or categories of training:

General Training. Refers to training that develops all-around fitness. Thus, general cardiovascular or endurance training, for many individuals, would be performing 20 minutes of aerobic activity such as stationary bicycling or running. General strength training refers to weight training that develops all the major muscle groups (including at least one exercise for each group) and bolsters overall strength capabilities. This type of training would normally make up the majority of activity during the off-season and early pre-season or preparation phase.

Sport-Specific Training. As the name implies, this type of training refers to physical conditioning or skill work specific to a particular sport. For example, for a 100-meter sprinter this could mean performing repeat 50-meter sprints in an interval training format. For a basketball player, it would refer to specific jumping and lateral movement drills similar to the jumping and lateral movements needed to be successful in the game.

Sport-specific weight training would include exercises that develop muscular characteristics (e.g., power) and strengthen muscle groups necessary for success in a particular sport. For the 100-meter sprinter, this would mean exercises that strengthen and improve the power of the thighs, the lower legs, and the hip musculature. For a discus thrower, it would mean exercises that improve the power and strengthen the legs and hip musculature; the upper body musculature; and the torso muscles that rotate the upper body in relation to the lower body. But whatever the sport, the goal of sport-specific training is to train the muscles in a fashion similar to how they'll be used during the actual competitive situation. Thus, for many sports this would mean power-oriented training.

Sport-specific training also includes direct skill training for the sport in question. Thus, for basketball, shooting drills would come under the heading of such training; and for baseball, hitting drills would be sport-specific. This type of training would be included in training phases that are relatively close to the onset of competition and during the actual season itself. Such training phases are the late off-season, pre-season, in-season, late preparation, first transition, and competition phases.

Competition-Specific Training. Here the athlete is placed in a situation very similar to the actual sport or competition setting. Thus, scrimmages in basketball or football would constitute competition-specific training. In powerlifting, performing mock meets prior to a major competition would be another example of competition-specific training. In bodybuilding, practicing a posing routine would be competition-specific training. Such training also includes things like playing crowd noise over the loudspeakers of a football stadium or basketball arena while conducting practice drills, so that athletes become accustomed to the ambiance and the specific environment they will face in competition. Competition-specific training would be undertaken predominately during the late pre-season, in-season, or competition training phases.

STRENGTH/POWER PERIODIZATION, AMERICAN-STYLE

American coaches, developing their own terminology to describe a periodized training program, tended to come from a background of strength/power sports such as Olympic weightlifting and throwing events in track and field. Therefore, it must always be remembered that said terminology (and the attendant program type) was developed for a strength/power athlete and not a bodybuilder, distance runner, or any other type of athlete outside the power sports realm. Fortunately, the ideas contained within this periodized program can be applied to virtually any individual's training (Figure 4.2).

Similar to the original traditional European periodized plan, this schema was originally designed to prepare an athlete for one major competition a year, such as national championships. Thus, originally, each training phase lasted several months. However, it became apparent that if each training phase were in fact shorter in length, greater gains could be made over the course of an entire training year. Therefore, each training phase was shortened to as little as four weeks, and the periodized plan simply repeated several times throughout the training year. Similar to the traditional European plan, this plan begins with a high-volume/low-intensity phase and ends with a high-intensity/low-volume phase.

The last training phase emphasizes maximal power and strength for one repetition. This is because, for most strength power type sports—such as weightlifting or shot putting—maximal strength and power on a one-rep basis is what is needed to be successful. Raw power explodes from this successful periodization regimen!

Figure 4.2

PERIODIZATION TABLE FOR STRENGTH/POWER SPORT*

	Hypertrophy	Strength	Power	Peaking	Active Rest
Sets	3-4	3-5	3-5	1-3	Other Activities
Reps	8-20	2-6	2-3	1-3	
Volume	High	Med-High	Low	Very Low	
Intensity	Low	High	High	Very High	

*Adapted from Fleck and Kraemer, *Designing Resistance Training Programs*

Hypertrophy Phase. The goal of this phase is to develop muscle mass and size (or hypertrophy) to support the development of strength and power in subsequent training phases. Training consists of a relatively high volume (8-20 repetitions per set) at a low-to-moderate intensity. For many athletes, especially weight-class athletes, a secondary goal could be to reduce percentage of body fat.

Strength Phase. The goal is to develop basic strength and serve as a transition between the hypertrophy phase and the power phase. Compared to the hypertrophy phase, the volume (2-6 repetitions per set) is decreased and the intensity is increased.

Power Phase. This phase was designed to optimize the development and expression of true maximal strength and power. Therefore, the intensity is very high and the volume of training low (2-3 repetitions per set). This allows the individual to recover physiologically from the previous high-volume training and to prepare psychologically for the maximal and near-maximal efforts necessary for this mode of training.

Peaking Phase. This phase is undertaken right before a major competition. The volume is very low and the intensity very high (1-3 repetitions per set). The goal is to prepare the athlete for the truly maximal efforts needed for an actual competition—including epic struggles like Olympic weightlifting and grueling throwing events in track and field.

Active Rest Phase. Similar to its counterpart in the traditional European periodized plan, this phase allows the individual to recover psychologically and physiologically from previous training phases. During this phase, light weight training and activities unlike those the athlete generally competes in are performed. Although originally up to several months in length, this phase is now commonly only one to two weeks long.

REPETITION MAXIMUM

Common to all three types of terminology is the use of repetition maximum (RM) resistances or weights. *An RM is a weight that allows X but not X+1 repetitions in a set.* So a four repetition maximum is the maximal weight that can be used for four complete repetitions, but not five. A 10 RM is the heaviest weight that allows 10 complete reps, but not eleven. So a 4 RM is ipso facto heavier than a 10 RM.

The heaviest weight that can be used for one complete repetition with good exercise form and technique is 1 RM.

DETERMINING REPETITION MAXIMUM

Many periodization programs determine the weight used in various training phases as a percentage of a RM weight. For example, the program might call for performing six repetitions using 75% of 1 RM; or performing 12 repetitions using 90% of the 12 RM weight.

You can determine any RM weight from 1 to 25 RM by following these steps:

1. Warm up with five to 10 repetitions using 50 percent of an estimated RM.
2. After a minute or two of rest and some stretching, use 70 percent of that estimated RM to perform the desired number of repetitions—i.e., if you're looking to find your 1 RM, do one rep; if you're looking to find your 10 RM, do ten reps.

3. Repeat step two, only now you're using 90% of the estimated RM.
4. After two minutes or so of rest, again repeat step two, this time using 100 to 105 percent of the estimated RM.
5. If step four is successfully completed, repeat step two, rest included, this time using one to five percent more weight than you used in step four.
6. If you successfully complete step five, repeat the entire cycle after at least one full day of rest, starting with a heavier weight in step one.

Again, the RM weight is the heaviest weight with which the desired number of repetitions can be performed.

So there we have the basic terminology of periodization, and the breakdown of actual training designations. Now you have a basic idea of how training volume and intensity can be planned for an entire training year, or one complete training cycle. This information will be used in the following chapters to outline and design an actual training session, training month, training week—right down to a single session.

As we begin the practical application, make sure you've thoroughly digested all the info from these first four chapters. Know what you're talking about and you'll know what you're doing.

SELECTED READINGS:
• Bompa, T.O. Theory and Methodology of Training: The Key to Athletic Performance. 3rd edition, Kendall/Hunt Publishing Co., Dubuque, IA, 1994.
• Fleck, S.J. and W.J. Kraemer. Designing Resistance Training Programs. Human Kinetics, Publishers, Champaign, IL, 1987.
• Matveyev, L. Fundamentals of Sports Training. Progress Publishers, Moscow, 1977.

CHAPTER 5

periodization models

eriodization models refer to variations in training that have yielded proven results in increased strength, power, muscle hypertrophy, and athletic performance. As discussed in chapter 4, the typical training pattern is to increase intensity and decrease training volume as a competition nears. In addition, the volume of skill training and specific competition strategies also increase. As depicted in Figure 4.1, intensity normally peaks slightly before a major competition, allowing a recovery period prior to competition that will help lead to maximal performance skills. Skill type training should also peak slightly before competition—actually, even slightly closer to the competition than does intensity. Similar to the intensity pattern, there will be that short recovery period between the peak in skill training volume and actual competition.

Major Training Phases Within a Year. We're going to present several models of yearly major training phases. Weekly periodization patterns will also be delineated. Some European terminology will be used, such as macrocycle (yearly phase); mesocycle (monthly or major training phase); and microcycle (weekly phase). See the prior chapter if you need to clarify or review any periodization terminology.

In addition, the planning and arrangement of daily training sessions will also be discussed. It is important to remember that although the models presented do result in increases in strength, power, muscle size, and athletic performance, that the very concept of periodization is rooted in training variation. Variegated training takes a seemingly infinite number of forms, and is limited only by the creativity of the individual designing the program.

Yearly Models. The most common pattern of training intensity, volume, and skill training is seen throughout a year of training as presented in Figure 4.1. As noted, it is a pattern of increasing training intensity and decreasing training volume as a major competition approaches. However, this does not mean that intensity is constantly increasing and volume constantly decreasing. While the pattern of training volume and intensity presented in Figure 5.1., Strength Power Yearly Plan or Macrocycle, is also one of increasing intensity and decreasing volume prior to competition, in this plan there are wave-like patterns in both volume and intensity throughout the training year. However, this ebb-and-flow pattern does not contradict the greater overall pattern.

In addition, the training year, or macrocycle, is composed of four mesocycles, or training phases. Each training phase likewise has a wave-like pattern of decreasing volume and increasing intensity as the end of the phase approaches. This is key because, as previously stated, it has become apparent that several patterns of increasing intensity and decreasing volume throughout a training year have been shown to be more effective than one long pattern (a year in length).

There are three recovery periods within the total training year. These occur at the end of a training phase. Within each recovery period, training volume and intensity are both relatively low compared to the training immediately preceding the recovery period. Even so, recovery periods are very important, allowing the athlete to recoup both physiologically and psychologically, and minimizing the possibility of injury and overtraining.

Figure 5.1. Strength power yearly plan or macrocycle.

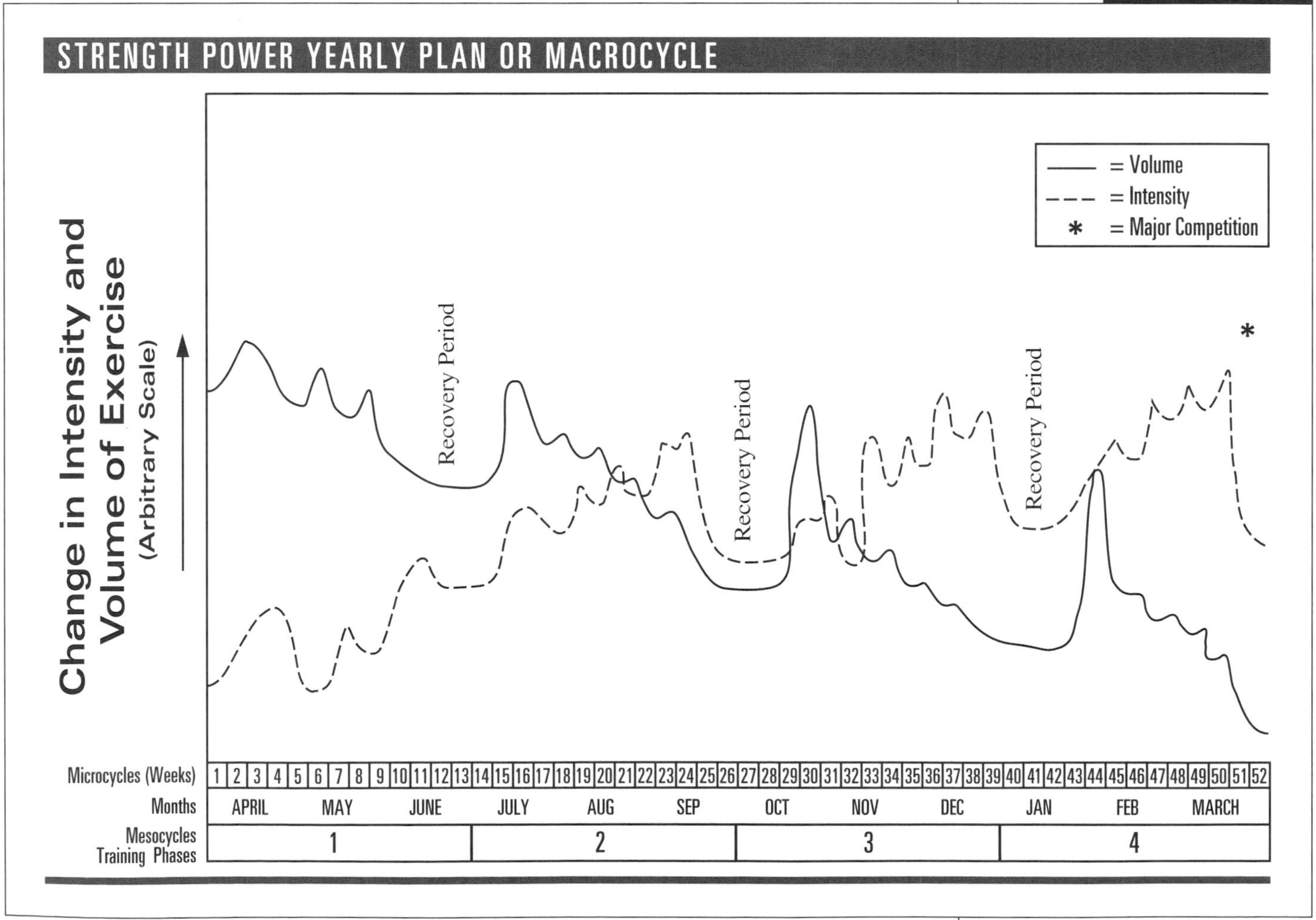

The set and repetition pattern for each mesocycle within the strength power yearly training plan might be quite similar to the American strength power training plan presented in Table 4.1. Thus, each major training segment would began with a hypertrophy phase and end with a strength power phase.

The general pattern of 3-4 major training phases per year as seen in Figure 5.1—with each beginning with relatively high volume and low intensity, and ending with relatively high intensity and low volume—can be applied to a myriad of sports and activities. However, the number of sets per exercise, repetitions per set, choice of exercise, and training sessions per week would be varied to meet the strength, power, and local muscular endurance needs of the particular sport.

Periodization is all about meeting specific training needs. As an example, if the sport being trained were not a true strength power sport, but a strength endurance sport—such as the 400-meter event in track and field—the same general pattern of training intensity and volume could be maintained with changes in the number of sets, repetitions, and training days per week. For an event such as the 400-meters in track and field, the first mesocycle could consist of 15-20 repetitions per set and 2-3 sets of each exercise; then progress to 5-8 repetitions per set with 2-3 sets of each exercise. Thus, the training intensity would increase for this type of event. However, resistance training might be performed only 2-3 times per week. Prior to the major competition, resistance training might not be performed at all for a period of 2-3 weeks. This allows more training time to be dedicated to de facto sprint and track work prior to actual competition. It also allows adequate recovery so that peak performance can be achieved.

A year's training plan for a team sport such as collegiate football is presented in Figure 5.2. Familiarly, the first mesocycle is made up of relatively high-volume/low-intensity exercise, again to develop muscle hypertrophy and basic strength and power levels. During spring training, the volume and intensity of resistance training is relatively low. Immediately after spring training, a short recovery period of low-intensity/low-volume weight training is undertaken. The first part of mesocycle two consists of relatively high-volume exercise at a moderate intensity.

The second part of mesocycle two consists of higher intensity and lower-volume exercise, so that maximal strength and power can be developed in preparation for the season. In-season training consists of moderate intensity and moderate-volume resistance training. The goal of the in-season program is to maintain the strength power levels developed during mesocycle one and two.

In sum, the goal of the entire yearly training program is to develop hypertrophy, strength, and power prior to the season, and then maintain these gains during the season. This type of training plan is applicable to many sports with relatively long in-season phases—such as baseball, ice hockey, basketball, and volleyball.

TRAINING PHASE PERIODIZATION

Now we know that training phases or mesocycles begin with a relatively high training volume and low training intensity, and as they progress, training intensity increases and training volume decreases. But note how Figures 5.3 to 5.6 depict sev-

Figure 5.2

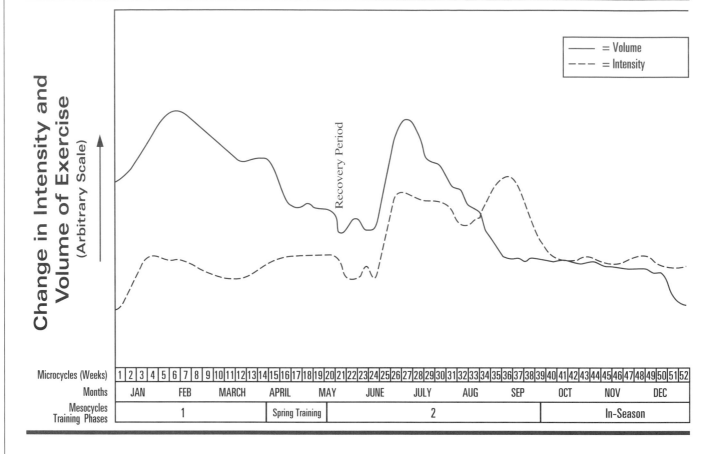

TEAM SPORT YEARLY PLAN OR MACROCYCLE

Figure 5.2. Team sport yearly plan or macrocycle.

eral variations of training volume and intensity within a four-week training phase. Training phases can also be longer than four weeks. In that case, the numbers one through four in the Figures could represent distinct periods of time within a phase that are longer than one week.

As an example, if the training phase was eight weeks in length the one, two, three, and four could represent time periods of two weeks. In addition, it is not imperative that all cycles within a training phase be exactly the same length. Because one of the keys to continued gains is variation in training, it is important that the training be varied in some manner in every one to two week period. No, this does not mean that the training program must be totally redesigned every one to two weeks—but some change in the training should be made on a regular basis.

Common changes made during a training phase include all the factors that were described in chapter 3, "What Can be Changed?" To review: common changes made within any training phase include altering the intensity of training (by increasing and decreasing the weight); changing the volume by increasing or decreasing the sets and repetitions; and changing the length of rest periods between sets and exercises.

Another common change made within a mesocycle is to vary the exercises. The most common pattern for many strength power sports and team sports is to perform more power-oriented exercises as the training phase progresses. Little or no plyometric training would be included during the beginning of a training phase. As the end of the phase approached, a greater volume of plyometric type training would be included. Other variations include changes in the exercises for a particular body part or muscle group. Such as doing hammer curls early on in the training phase and changing to concentration curls near the end of a mesocycle (thereby training different portions of the elbow flexors).

It's also worth stressing one more time that all changes in your regimen should be made with concrete training goals in mind, and never on a strictly random basis for the sheer sake of variety.

Figure 5.3 depicts a "step approach" for increasing intensity and decreasing volume during the first three weeks of a training phase. The fourth week is a recovery week in which training intensity is medium and volume low. This step approach, followed by a recovery period, is one of the most common patterns within a training phase.

Figure 5.4 depicts a training plan with two high-intensity weeks in the middle of the phase. The period of high-intensity training is followed by a recovery week at the end.

Figure 5.5 outlines a plan with two weeks of high-intensity training at the end of the phase. This type of plan is normally undertaken during the pre-season or preparatory phase of training. During such phases, a recovery period may not be needed at the end, because it does not lead into actual competition.

Figure 5.6 delineates a variation of volume and intensity employed during a phase specifically designed to taper before a competition. The phase begins with two weeks of high intensity and medium or low-volume training, followed by a third week of medium intensity and low-volume training. The phase ends with a recovery period during which little or no resistance training is performed. Competition would take place after the fourth week of the program.

WEEKLY PERIODIZATION

Weekly or microcycle periodization refers to variations of training within one training week. In general, high intensity or high-volume days should be followed by days of complete rest, or days comprised of low-to-medium intensity and volume. Light training days are necessary to allow recovery from heavy days. Other common changes made on a weekly basis include variations in exercises and exercise order.

Figure 5.7 depicts a common variation in training intensity and volume during weekly periodization. It consists of one day of high, medium, and low-intensity training, all at medium volume. This type of weekly variation is commonly used by individuals performing a total body workout each training day. An agenda for such a weekly plan would be to perform three sets of each exercise at 100% of 10 RM for 10 repetitions on Monday; three sets of each exercise at 80-85% of 10 RM for 10 repetitions on Wednesday; and three sets of each exercise at 90% of 10 RM for 10 repetitions on

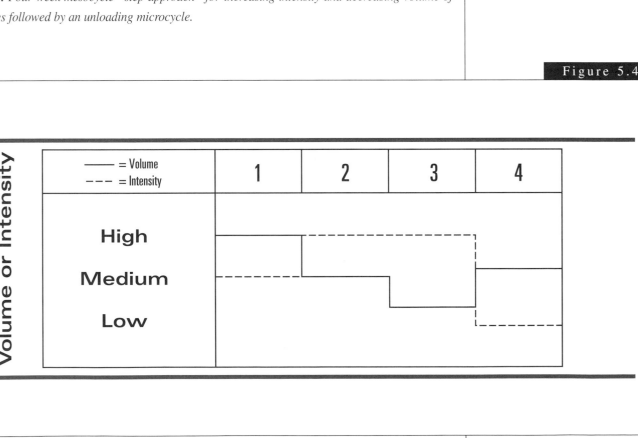

Figure 5.3

Figure 5.3. *Four-week mesocycle "step approach" for increasing intensity and decreasing volume of microcycles followed by an unloading microcycle.*

Figure 5.4

Figure 5.4. *Four-week mesocycle of two high-intensity microcycles followed by a recovery microcycle.*

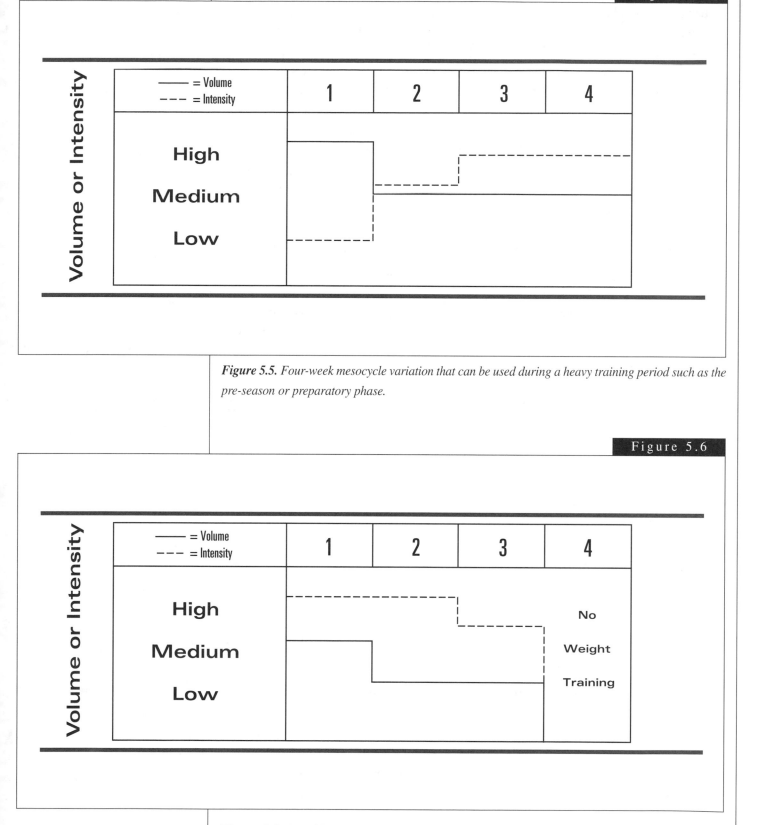

Figure 5.5. Four-week mesocycle variation that can be used during a heavy training period such as the pre-season or preparatory phase.

Figure 5.6. Possible variation in volume and intensity during a mesocycle designed to taper for a competition.

Friday. Note that the high-intensity training day is preceded by two days of rest on Saturday and Sunday and is followed by a light day of training on Wednesday. This should allow sufficient recovery between high-intensity days so that ongoing progress can be made.

A common problem encountered when doing a total body workout on three training days per week is that all training sessions may be performed at a very high intensity. This quickly leads to a training plateau—a frustrating lack of further gains. But there's a viable solution. Variation of training intensity will result in sufficient rest between sessions and sufficient training stimulus for continued gains.

Figure 5.8 depicts the intensity and volume pattern for a week of very heavy training, consisting of three training sessions per week of a high intensity and low-volume nature—with two of the high-intensity sessions performed on consecutive days. There are also two days of medium intensity and medium volume within the week. After the substantial training undertaken on Monday through Friday, Saturday is a light day of low volume and medium intensity, and Sunday is a complete recovery day. This type of weekly variation can be used for short periods of time (three to four weeks) within a training phase. Such a heavy training period could be followed by a recovery week consisting primarily of working out medium-to-low volume and intensity. The recov-

Figure 5.7

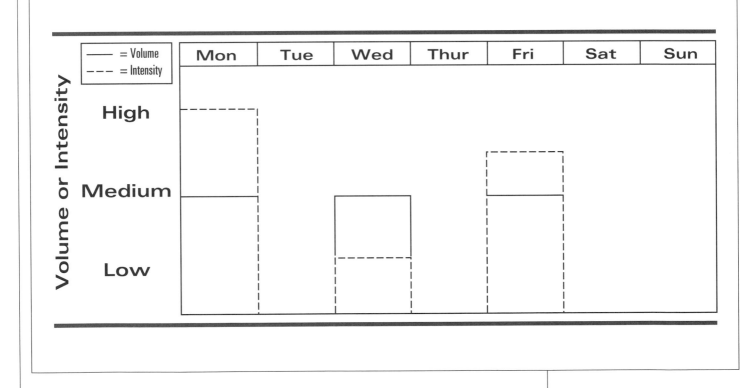

Figure 5.7. Common microcycle variation of high, medium and low-intensity days of training, all at a medium volume.

ery week would be necessary to ensure a physiological/psychological recoup from what has gone before, and prior to starting another period of medium-to-heavy training.

Figure 5.9 depicts weekly variations for an advanced bodybuilding program. It consists of two thigh and calf training days; two arm, shoulder training days; and two back and chest training days per week. One thigh and calf day is at a high volume and medium intensity; and the other at a high intensity and medium volume. The same is true for the arm/shoulder and back/chest training days. Abdominal work is performed two days per week with the same volume/intensity pattern. Training days for each body part are separated by at least two days, thus allowing sufficient recovery per body part. Sunday is a complete day of rest/recovery.

Other variations can be incorporated into the program. Thigh/leg exercises on Monday might include back squats, knee extensions, seated knee curls, standing calf raises, and seated calf raises. Thursday thigh/leg exercises might consist of leg press, back squats, standing knee curls, knee extensions, seated calf raises, and donkey calf raises.

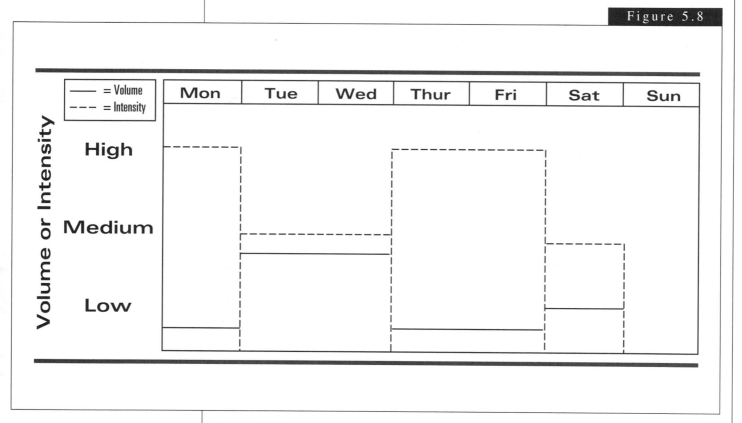

Figure 5.8 *Microcycle variation for use during a very heavy training period.*

The high-intensity day for a particular body part might consist of 3-4 sets of 6-8 repetitions at a 6-8 RM for each exercise, with 1-1/2 to 2 minute rests between sets and exercises. The medium intensity, high-volume day of training per body part might consist of 5-6 sets per exercise of 10-12 repetitions per set at a 10-12 repetition maximum, with a one-minute rest period between sets and exercises. Longer rest periods on high-intensity days allow more recovery so that the heavier weight can be handled for the prescribed number of repetitions. The exact same weekly variation is typically not per

Figure 5.9

	Mon	Tue	Wed	Thur	Fri	Sat	Sun
High							
Medium							
Low	Legs-Calves Thighs	Arms-Shoulders Abdominals	Back-Chest	Legs-Calves Thighs	Arms-Shoulders Abdominals	Back-Chest Abdominals	

— = Volume
--- = Intensity

Volume or Intensity (vertical axis)

Figure 5.9. Advanced bodybuilding microcycle with a high intensity/medium volume and a medium intensity/high-volume training day for all body parts.

formed more than two or three times within a training phase. This is to ensure sufficient variation for continued—and theoretically, continuous—fitness gains.

PLANNING ONE SESSION

Virtually any factor that can be manipulated must be considered when designing one periodized training session. It is important that each training session be planned with the utmost care, because individual training sessions are the building blocks of both a weekly training phase and a yearly training plan. Poorly designed individual training sessions inevitably result in a poorly designed yearly training program, and therefore less than optimal fitness gains.

All the general factors discussed in chapter 3 must be considered when designing one training session. Let's take this opportunity to go into these factors in a little more depth.

Exercise order can be decided upon by prioritizing your exercises. This means that exercises emphasizing a weakness of the trainee or those emphasizing muscle groups necessary for success in a particular sporting activity are performed early in the training session. A bodybuilder whose success is limited by a lack of quadriceps musculature might hit their quads early in the session. This will ensure that the quad exercises can be performed at the desired intensity and volume, and thus result in gains in muscular size and definition.

An athlete whose performance is limited by thigh/leg strength and power—such as a high-jumper or long-jumper—might perform the majority of thigh/leg exercises early in a session, prior to any upper body exercises.

A corollary of priority arrangement of exercises is that, generally speaking, power type exercises should be performed early in a training session. Exercises such as plyometrics, or power cleans, snatch pulls, or weighted jumps, should be completed with maximal power, before fatigue sets in. Maximal effort when power training is necessary for success in many sports and activities.

Exercises emphasizing muscle groups and joints either already injured, or susceptible to injury, need to be included in the training. The most common injury sites are the knee, ankle, shoulder, and lower back. Such exercises are especially useful during the off-season preparatory phase of training. For sports which have a very long in-season, exercises emphasizing easily-injured muscle groups and joints should be included in the in-season program as well. Injury can easily occur due to loss of strength in these muscle groups during a lengthy season.

Recall again that it can also be desirable to vary such factors as the number of sets performed; the number of repetitions performed; and the rest periods between sets and exercises. If an athlete's success in sports such as a basketball or volleyball is limited by upper body strength and power more so than lower body strength, the training session should be clearly designed with this in mind. Thus, a training session in the off-season preparatory phase for such an athlete might consist of 4-5 sets of each upper body exercise and only three sets per lower body exercise. Know your priorities!

If a bodybuilder's success is limited by a lack of symmetry between upper and lower body musculature—with say the lower body less developed—this should be seriously considered when designing periodized training sessions. In order to correct the problem, you'll employ more lower body part exercises, and more sets per lower body exercise. In addition, it might also lead to 30 second to one-minute rest intervals between lower body sets and exercises, as opposed to 1-1/2 to two-minute rest periods between upper body sets and exercises. Such manipulations should, over time, result in greater hypertrophy of the lower body, satisfying your quest for superior symmetry.

Generally speaking, individuals like to perform exercises in which they've already gained proficiency, and tend to avoid those they perform relatively poorly. But often, exercises a trainee tends to avoid may be those same exercises he or she should be looking to incorporate into his or her training sessions. (This line of reasoning is only valid when one presumes that the trainee does not have an injury that precludes the performance of certain exercises.)

Overall, the two most vital questions to ask are: What are the goals of the training session? And, what are the needs of the trainee? Unless these questions are sufficiently addressed early on, you are not going to succeed in any great measure when it comes to achieving your periodized training goals.

MULTIPLE TRAINING SESSIONS ON THE SAME DAY

One possible way to increase training intensity and volume within one day's training is to undertake multiple training sessions. If more than one training session is attempted on the same day, the recovery period between sessions means they can be performed with very high intensity, when compared to performing the same volume of training in a single session. Also, if more than one training session is performed on the same day, a greater number of exercises and/or sets can be added, resulting in greater total volume, if such is your desire. Time and scheduling constraints might also make shorter, multiple training sessions more applicable to your hectic, every-minute-counts lifestyle. If you do a lot of lifting in your routine—or plan to get involved in competitive bodybuilding or powerlifting—then multiple training sessions become even more appealing.

But whatever your reason for favoring multiple sessions, it should be remembered that sufficient time *must* be allowed to adapt to an increase in training intensity or volume. Therefore, if two training sessions per day are built into your program, the additional session should be added gradually. Here's a specific training example: when first starting your two training periods per day, only one or two training days per week should incorporate the two sessions for a period of two to three weeks. Additional two-sessions days can be slowly incorporated until the desired number of multiple training days are achieved. For each additional twice-a-day session added to the program, an adaptation period of two to three weeks should be allowed.

Important question: does increasing total training volume and intensity using multiple daily training sessions lead to overtraining? Can athletes safely and effectively tolerate multiple training sessions? These questions have been investigated—and answered—in a series of sport science studies using elite Olympic weightlifters as subjects. It is apparent that when Olympic-style weightlifters perform a training session in both the morning and the afternoon of the same day, strength decreases after the first training session. However, it is recovered by the second session (Häkkinen, 1992; Häkkinen, et al., 1988a). The strength of Olympic-style weightlifters also recovers between training sessions when two sessions are performed on the same day on four out of seven days (Häkkinen, et al., 1988b). It is apparent therefore that—at least for Olympic-style weightlifters—strength levels can recover, and gains in strength levels be made when two training sessions per day are undertaken for short periods of time.

Still, indicators of overwork must be carefully monitored. If the lifter starts to use improper exercise technique in order to finish a workout; cannot complete a training session that previously had been completed; or shows any other indication of overwork—the intensity and/or volume should be decreased so that an overtraining syndrome does not occur.

As a two-session-a-day trainee, you can maintain very high training intensity by performing the same total training volume, but dividing the volume in half between an afternoon and morning training session. This strategy to keep training intensity high has successfully been used by Olympic weightlifters (Häkkinen and Pakarinen, 1991).

In this study, Olympic lifters over a two-week period completed only one training session per day; and in another two-week period performed two training sessions per day. The total training volume (exercises, sets, weights, and repetitions) was exactly the same during each two-week period. The only difference was that during the period when two training sessions per day were performed, the training volume was equally divided between a morning and afternoon session. Measures taken during and after each two-week training period indicated that the lifter's strength increased to a slightly greater extent during the period of two training sessions per day. It appears—at least among elite athletes, that the strategy of dividing the volume between two sessions can result in greater strength increases.

To summarize the key points of this chapter: there are many possible training variations that can be incorporated into any training program phase—be it yearly, monthly, weekly, daily, or whatever. But the training goals and needs of the individual must always be kept in mind when planning a program.

The next chapter discusses the importance of keeping a record of your well-designed periodization program.

SELECTED READINGS:

• Bompa, T.P. (1994). Theory and Methodology of Training: The Key to Athletic Performance. Kendall/Hunt Publishing Co., Dubuque, IA.

• Fleck, S.J. and Kraemer, W.J. (1987). Designing Resistance Training Programs. Human Kinetics Publishing, Champaign, IL.

• Häkkinen, K. (1992). Neuromuscular responses in male and female athletes to two successive strength training sessions in one day. Journal of Sports Medicine Physical Fitness, 32, 234-242.

• Häkkinen, K., Alen, M. and Komi, P.V. (1985a). Changes in isometric force and relaxation time,electromyographic and muscle fiber characteristics of human skeletal muscle during strength training and detraining. Acta Physiologica Scandinavica, 125, 573-585.

• Häkkinen, K. and Komi, P.V. (1988b). Changes in electrical and mechanical behavior of leg extensor muscles during heavy resistance strength training. Scandinavian Journal of Sports Science, 7, 65-76.

• Häkkinen, K. and Pakarinen, A. (1991). Serum hormones in male strength athletes during intensive short term strength training. European Journal of Applied Physiology, 63, 194-199.

keeping records

ave you ever seen someone in the middle of their workout, scratching their head and looking at the weight stack on a machine as if to say, "Now, what weight did I use last time?" Sure you have! Gyms are full-up with slightly befuddled individuals. Knowing the weight used for an exercise, repetitions per set, and sets performed in previous training sessions are some of the reasons for keeping a training record.

The information contained in a training record is invaluable for:

- knowing what has been done in previous training sessions;
- seeing progress from training session to training session;
- having an accurate record of what was performed during a successful training program;
- having an accurate record of a training program that did not work so that it is not repeated and can be corrected;
- making small changes in a previously successful program to make it even more successful;
- knowing when it is time to make a change in training volume or intensity.

Keeping an accurate training record makes it *de rigeur* that your sessions be planned *before* entering the gym. This is important because it allows sufficient time to carefully plan the training program. Although minor changes in a program can be made at any time—including when you are in the gym—it is very important that the training program not be planned based upon what you see other individuals doing in the gym on any particular day. Nor should you plan the second half of a training session based entirely upon how you feel after the first half of a session. An accurate training record means that the training sessions are carefully planned and allows for constant evaluation of the program on a consistent basis.

There are two major ways of accurately keeping a training record. One method uses a printed workout card (as presented in Figure 6.1); and the other consists of a handwritten record kept in a notebook (as presented in Figure 6.3). The example printed workout card has sufficient space for planning four training sessions. Each session has space for 10 exercises and three sets of each exercise. In addition, the upper left-hand box (the one with no diagonal line)—next to the box where the name of the exercise is filled in—can be used to indicate the planned number of sets, repetitions, and intended weight to be used. The boxes with the diagonal lines are where the actual weight used and number of repetitions performed are recorded. At the bottom of the page is a place to indicate any comments concerning the training session.

Figure 6.2 is what the training card would look like when completely filled out, including, among other things, the planned exercises, repetitions, sets, and weights to be used in the training session. The dates of the training sessions, as well as whether the session was light, moderate, or heavy in nature, has been indicated. The number of repetitions and weights actually used for each set during a training session and some comments about the session have also been filled in for two training sessions. On this training card, the place above the diagonal line is where the weight used in pounds for the exercises is indicated. While the space below the line is used to record the number of repetitions actually performed.

The use of a printed training card does allow one to keep an accurate record of each training session. However, it is not necessary to use such a card. Many people find the use of a training notebook just as easy when it comes to keeping accurate records of each session. An example of a training session record from a notebook is shown in Figure 6.3. The date of the training session, planned exercises, planned number of sets, repetitions per set, weights to be used for the exercises, and the number of sets and repetitions actually performed during the training session are indicated by the notations to the right of each exercise.

As an example, for the leg press, the notation 3x8 @ 200 pounds indicates that it was planned to perform three sets each of eight repetitions using 200 pounds. The notation 3x8, 8, 8 indicates that for the leg press, three sets each of eight repetitions were actually performed during the training session. As can be seen from the record for the bench press, it was planned to perform three sets each of eight repetitions using 150 pounds. However, the record of what actually transpired during the session indicates that, for the bench press, three sets were performed, but the last two sets consisted of seven repetitions rather than eight.

Figure 6.1

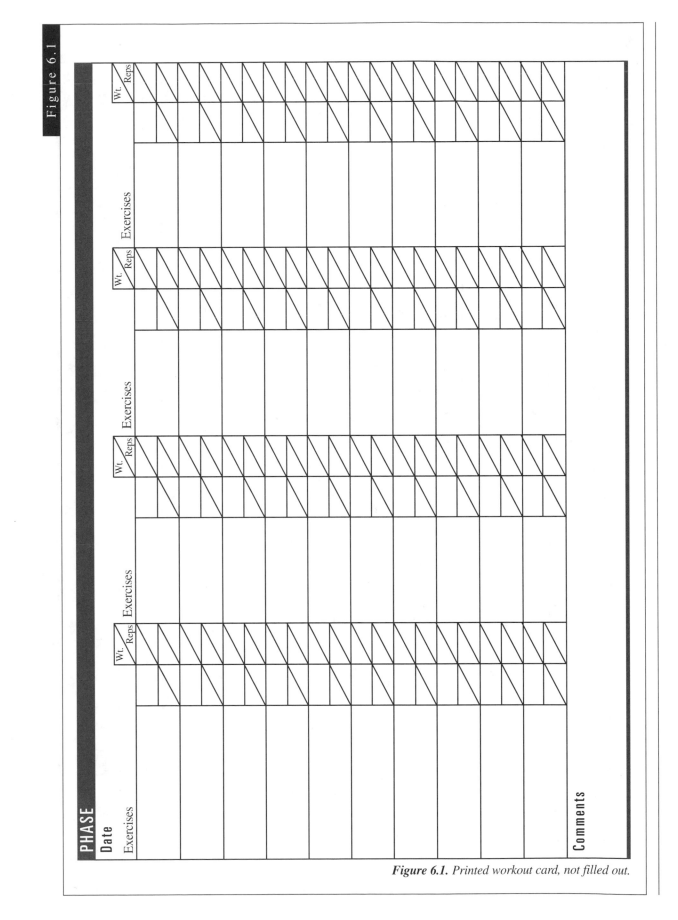

Figure 6.1. *Printed workout card, not filled out.*

Figure 6.2

PHASE: PREPARATION

Date February 24, Mon (H)

Exercises	Wt.	Reps
Back Squat	100% 8-10 RM	
	200	10
	200	10
	200	9
Knee Curl	100% 8-10 RM	
	60	10
	60	9
	60	8
Hip Adduction	100% 8-10 RM	
	50	10
	50	10
	50	8
Hip Abduction	100% 8-10 RM	
	40	10
	40	9
	40	8
Seated Calf Raise	100% 8-10 RM	
	70	10
	70	10
	70	10
Back Extension	3 x 15 @ BW	
	BW	15
	BW	15
Abdominals Crunch/Rev. Crunch	3 x 20 Bar @ BW	
	BW	20
	BW	20
	BW	20
Russian Twist	3 x 15 Each Side BW	
	BW	15
	BW	15

February 25, Tue (H)

Exercises	Wt.	Reps
Flat Bench Dumbbell Flye	100% 8-10 RM	
	45	10
	45	10
Upright Row	100% 8-10 RM	
	85	10
	85	8
Lat Pull Down	100% 8-10 RM	
	130	10
	130	8
Dumbbell Bent Over Row	100% 8-10 RM	9
	50	
	50	8
Rotator Cuff	3 x 10-12 Light Wt.	10
	10	12
	10	12
Triceps Press Down	100% 8-10 RM	
	70	10
	70	9
Dumbbell Biceps Curl	100% 8-10 RM	
	45	10
	45	9

February 28, Fri (M)

Exercises	Wt.	Reps
Lunge	95% 8-10 RM	
Knee Curl	95% 8-10 RM	
Hip Adduction	95% 8-10 RM	
Hip Adduction	95% 8-10 RM	
Seated Toe Raise	95% 8-10 RM	
Back Extension	3 x 15 @ BW	
Abdominals Crunch	3 x 20 @ BW	
Med Ball Twist	3 x 15 Each Side	

February 29, Sat (M)

Exercises	Wt.	Reps
Flat Bench Dumbbell Flye	95% 8-10 RM	
Lateral Dumbbell Raise	95% 8-10 RM	
Front Dumbbell Raise	95% 8-10 RM	
Wide Grip Pull Up	3 x 10-12 @ BW	
Seated Row	95% 8-10 RM	
Rotator Cuff	3 x 10-12 Light Wt.	
Dumbbell Biceps Curl	95% 8-10 RM	

Comments: Perform Educational Repetitions: of hang clean pulls (3 x 5 Lt. Wt.) and Romanian deadlift (3 x 5 Lt. Wt.) on days 1 & 2 (Mon & Thu) and pronate position cable row (3 x 5 Lt. Wt.) on days 2 & 4 (Tue & Fri) prior to regular exercises.

Figure 6.2. Filled-out printed workout card.

Figure 6.3

March 18, 1996	Planned Program	Workout Results
Leg Press	3 x 8 @ 200 lb	3 x 8, 8, 8
Bench Press	3 x 8 @ 150 lb	3 x 8, 7, 7
Knee Curl	3 x 10 @ 40 lb	3 x 10, 10, 10
Knee Extension	3 x 10 @ 60 lb	3 x 10, 9, 8
Arm Curl	3 x 10 @ 25 lb	3 x 10, 10, 10
Triceps Extension	3 x 10 @ 40 lb	3 x 10, 10, 9
Calf Raises	3 x 12 @ 200 lb	3 x 12, 12, 12
Crunches	3 x 20	3 x 20, 20, 20

Comments: Felt good, increase leg press to 210 lb next session.

Figure 6.3. *Notebook type training record.*

We can see that it is important not only to keep a record of what was intended to be performed during a training session, but also *to keep an accurate training record of what was actually performed.* This allows for useful, sometimes subtle changes in the program—such as if it's time to increase the weight used for a particular exercise, and so on.

Once you've established the all-important standard of accuracy, the methodology used to keep your training record is a matter of choice.

Chapters 7 through 10 give examples of planning a year of training; a major training phase; a week of training; and one training session. Good planning and a painstaking training record are very important for making optimal gains whether one year or a single session is being considered.

planning one year of training

planning one total year of training in advance may seem like an impossible task. However, it is not necessary—or advisable—to exactly plan every training session for the entire year when developing a yearly training plan. The goal of developing a yearly training plan is to outline, in general, the training goals, training intensity, and training volume for the entire year. All the concepts and information discussed in the previous chapters should be applied to your planning. If the process is broken down into several steps, it's not as complicated as it may seem. Using a form similar to that presented in Figure 7.1, and following the basic steps listed below, will make the planning a painless if not a simple process.

The following steps should be followed when developing a general training plan for an entire year:

1. Write the month in which any major competitions of the year occur (e.g., state championships or national championships) in the space provided for months below the weeks or microcycles (49-52). These weeks correspond to the end of your training year. Then fill in the name and date of the major competition in the space provided near the top.

2. Working backwards from the major competition, fill in the dates and names of minor competitions—or if the sport has a season fill in the starting date and ending date of the season. Then write the appropriate months during which the minor competitions take place in the space provided below the weeks (1-52).

3. Fill in the months for the rest of the year, beginning with the month which immediately follows the month during which the major competitions fall. The month immediately after major competitions should be filled in under weeks one to four.

4. Determining the length of the season (the time period between minor competitions and the major competition), generally outline the total number of training phases within the year by placing lines where one phase will begin and another will end in the mesocycle training goals space provided.

5. Designate terms such as increased muscle size, hypertrophy, local muscular endurance, basic strength, recovery, power, maintenance, peaking, etc., to describe the major goals of the strength training program through various months and training phases. Indicate them in the mesocycle training goals space. These goals can also be thought of as the names of the training phases (i.e., strength training phase, etc.).

6. Indicate low, moderate, high, or very high training intensity and volume in the spaces provided. Intensity and volume must be appropriate for the goals of each training phase.

7. Generally outline the volume and intensity curves for the entire training year, following the schema developed in the intensity, volume, and training phase goals outlined in steps 5 and 6. It is not necessary that every little increase and decrease in intensity or volume be outlined in these general curves. The idea is to get a general training plan and not plan each and every increase or decrease in intensity or volume within each month and week of training.

A general training plan for the entire year has now been developed. It is now time to take a critical look at the whole plan and determine whether it will result in an optimal performance at the major competition(s), meeting the goals, objectives, and needs of the individual or team it is designed for. Careful evaluation is an important and dynamic aspect in developing any training plan.

If, after careful consideration, it appears the plan will not result in optimal performance (let's say there's not enough rest included, or the training volume is too high), changes should then be made and the new plan designed and evaluated. The process of changing and evaluating the training plan is repeated until you are fully satisfied it meets your needs.

Figures 7.2, 7.3 and 7.4 depict three different kinds of yearly periodized training plans:

1) Periodization for a Strength/Power Sport. Figure 7.2 was developed for a strength/power athlete such as a shot-putter or discus thrower. The major competition for the strength/power athlete is the state track meet, which is preceded by a regional track meet, conference track meet, and dual meets. The plan divides the year into two major training cycles, each consisting of a hypertrophy phase, strength phase, and power phase. The major training cycles are all followed by a brief recovery phase. Immediately prior to the dual meet season is a brief high-volume training phase. The dual meet season is designated as a peaking phase. It consists of relatively low-volume

Figure 7.1

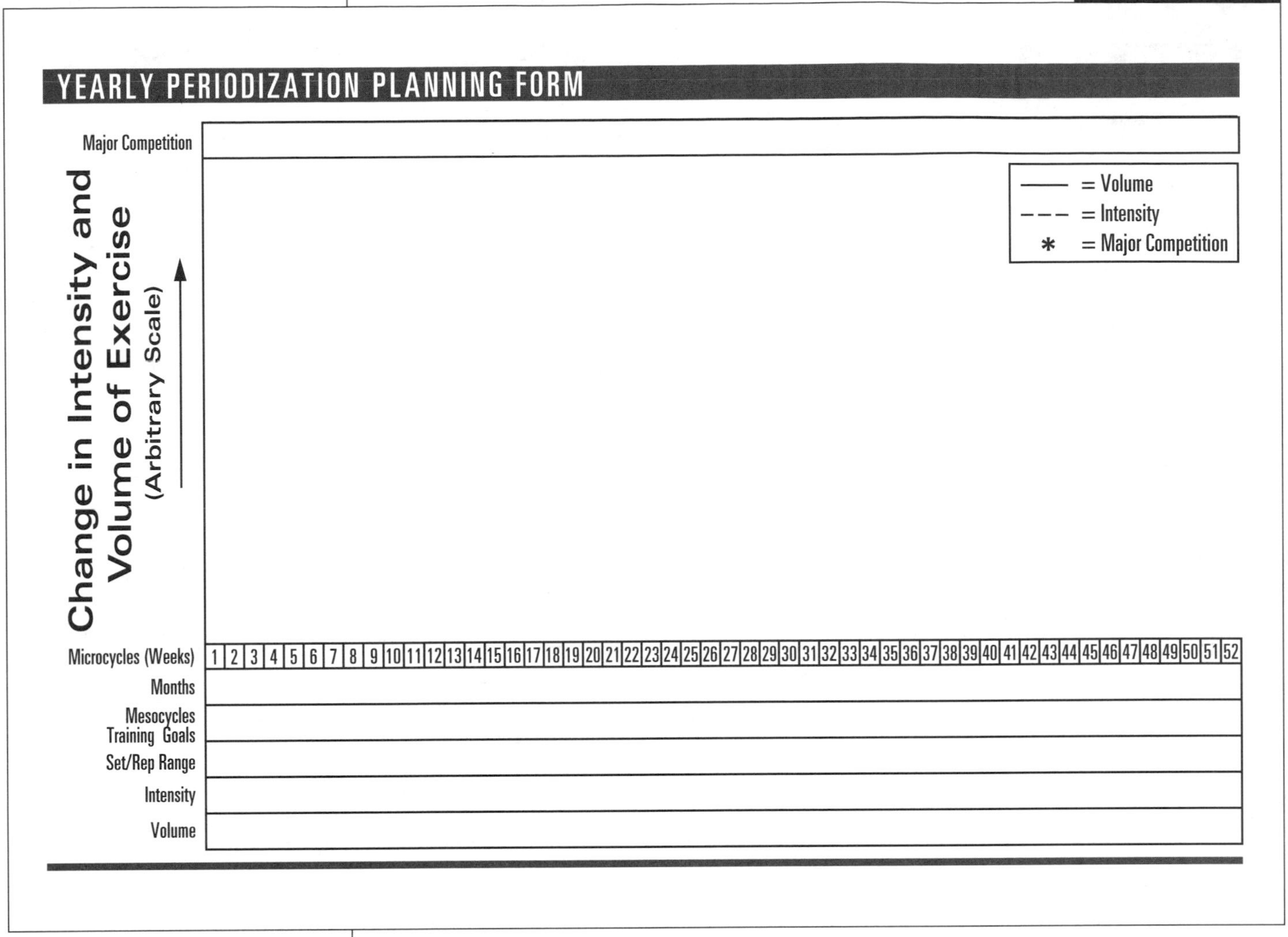

YEARLY PERIODIZATION PLANNING FORM

Major Competition

= Volume
= Intensity
* = Major Competition

Change in Intensity and
Volume of Exercise
(Arbitrary Scale)

Microcycles (Weeks) 1 2 3 4 5 6 7 8 9 10 11 12 13 14 15 16 17 18 19 20 21 22 23 24 25 26 27 28 29 30 31 32 33 34 35 36 37 38 39 40 41 42 43 44 45 46 47 48 49 50 51 52

Months

Mesocycles
Training Goals

Set/Rep Range

Intensity

Volume

Figure 7.1. Yearly periodization planning form.

and high-intensity resistance training. The competition phase during which the major meets take place consists of high-to-moderate intensity and low-volume resistance training. This plan should result in optimal performance during the competition phase of training in which the major meets take place.

2) Periodization Plan for Basketball. Figure 7.3 depicts the yearly training plan for a high school basketball player. The regional and state tournaments occur during March and are preceded by an in-season period of approximately three months. The plan consists of two major training cycles, each consisting of a hypertrophy and strength power-training phase. Immediately prior to the in-season is a period of high intensity, low-volume training. The two major training cycles of the year are separated by a brief two-week recovery period. The in-season maintenance program consists of moderate volume and moderate-intensity resistance training. The goal of the entire training plan is to develop strength and power prior to the start of the season and to maintain strength and power throughout the season.

Figure 7.2

PERIODIZATION PLAN FOR A STRENGTH/POWER SPORT

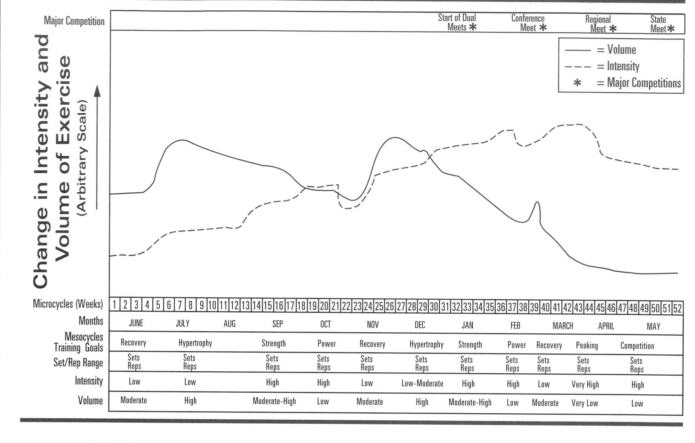

Microcycles (Weeks)	1 2 3 4 5 6 7 8 9 10 11 12 13 14 15 16 17 18 19 20 21 22 23 24 25 26 27 28 29 30 31 32 33 34 35 36 37 38 39 40 41 42 43 44 45 46 47 48 49 50 51 52										
Months	JUNE	JULY	AUG	SEP	OCT	NOV	DEC	JAN	FEB	MARCH	APRIL	MAY
Mesocycles Training Goals	Recovery	Hypertrophy	Strength	Power	Recovery	Hypertrophy	Strength	Power	Recovery	Peaking	Competition
Set/Rep Range	Sets Reps	Sets Reps	Sets Reps	Sets Reps	Sets Reps	Sets Reps	Sets Reps	Sets Reps	Sets Reps	Sets Reps	Sets Reps
Intensity	Low	Low	High	High	Low	Low-Moderate	High	High	Low	Very High	High
Volume	Moderate	High	Moderate-High	Low	Moderate	High	Moderate-High	Low	Moderate	Very Low	Low

Legend: —— = Volume; – – – = Intensity; * = Major Competitions

Major Competition: Start of Dual Meets *; Conference Meet *; Regional Meet *; State Meet *

Y-axis: Change in Intensity and Volume of Exercise (Arbitrary Scale)

Figure 7.2. *Periodization plan for strength/power sport.*

3) Periodization for General Fitness. The goal of many general fitness resistance trainers is to increase muscle mass and basic muscular strength. General fitness weight trainers may not have a competition to peak for. However, a well-designed periodization plan can aid the general fitness trainer in meeting their goals just the same. The training plan outlined consists of three major training cycles separated by two-week recovery periods. Each major training cycle consists of four training phases, each four weeks in length. The major goal of the first two phases in each of major training cycles is to increase muscle size. The major goal of the third phase is to increase muscle size and basic strength. While the goal of the fourth phase is to increase basic muscular strength. The first training phase in each major cycle consists of relatively low-intensity and high-volume training; the fourth phase in each major training cycle consists of relatively high-intensity and low-volume training. Therefore, each major training cycle follows the basic periodization premise of progressing from high-volume and low-intensity training to high-intensity and low-volume training. This plan should meet the goals of the general fitness weight trainer in more than adequate fashion.

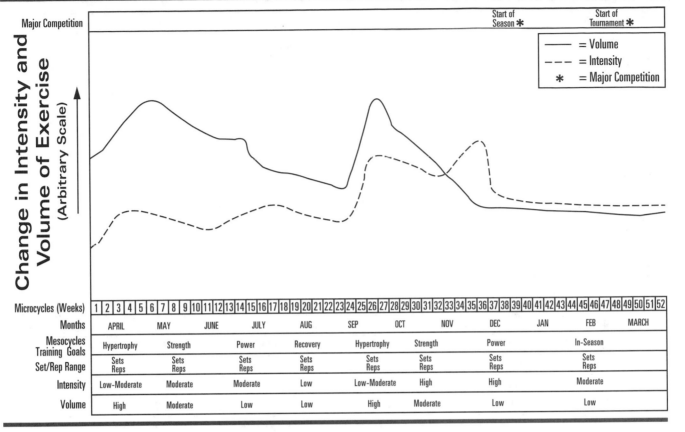

Figure 7.3. *Periodization plan for basketball.*

Now we've developed three different one-year periodization plans. In the next chapter, each training phase within these one-year plans will be developed even further.

Figure 7.4

PERIODIZATION PLAN FOR GENERAL FITNESS

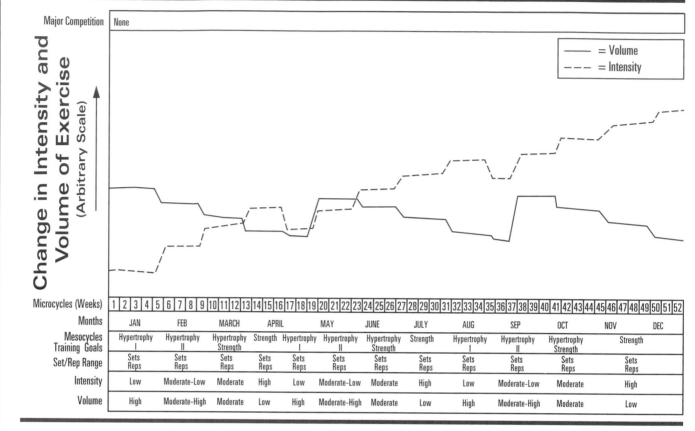

Major Competition: None

Legend: —— = Volume - - - = Intensity

Y-axis: Change in Intensity and Volume of Exercise (Arbitrary Scale)

Microcycles (Weeks)	1 2 3 4	5 6 7 8 9	10 11 12 13	14 15 16	17 18 19	20 21 22 23	24 25 26 27	28 29 30 31	32 33 34 35	36 37 38 39 40	41 42 43 44 45	46 47 48 49 50 51 52
Months	JAN	FEB	MARCH	APRIL	MAY	JUNE	JULY	AUG	SEP	OCT	NOV	DEC
Mesocycles Training Goals	Hypertrophy I	Hypertrophy II	Hypertrophy Strength	Strength	Hypertrophy I	Hypertrophy II	Hypertrophy Strength	Strength	Hypertrophy I	Hypertrophy II	Hypertrophy Strength	Strength
Set/Rep Range	Sets Reps	Sets Reps	Sets Reps	Sets Reps	Sets Reps	Sets Reps	Sets Reps	Sets Reps	Sets Reps	Sets Reps	Sets Reps	Sets Reps
Intensity	Low	Moderate-Low	Moderate	High	Low	Moderate-Low	Moderate	High	Low	Moderate-Low	Moderate	High
Volume	High	Moderate-High	Moderate	Low	High	Moderate-High	Moderate	Low	High	Moderate-High	Moderate	Low

Figure 7.4. Periodization plan for general fitness.

planning a mesocycle
or training phase

enerally planning a year of training does, to some extent, take into consideration the intensity and volume of each training phase.

Important information concerning training variations within each phase was discussed in chapter 5, "Periodization Models," and this clearly should be applied to your planning.

Look again at the examples of yearly training plans presented in Figures 7.2, 7.3, and 7.4. This basic plan includes the length, volume, and intensity of each training phase.

Now let's look to further develop each training phase. The outline provided in Figure 8.1—the training phase planning guide—will help you devise an even more detailed, sophisticated profile of each phase.

Starting at the top, let's discuss each segment of the planning guide:

Sport Activity. This simply refers to the discipline for which training is being planned. Examples include basketball, golf, baseball, racquetball, shot-putting, bodybuilding, soccer, or distance running.

Training Phase. This refers to the name of the phase. Many times a training phase is named for its major training goal. Training phase goals were included in Figures 7.2, 7.3, and 7.4. These major training goals would also constitute appropriate names for the actual phase. Thus, hypertrophy training phase; strength training phase; strength/power training phase, and so on.

Length of Training Phase. Refers to how long the phase will be, normally expressed in a matter of weeks.

Dates of Training Phase. The date on which the training phase will begin and end.

Training Goals. That is, the major training goals of each phase. Common goals include an increase in muscle size, strength, local muscular endurance, and muscle power. Increases in performance measures may also be a major training goal—such as an increase in vertical jump ability, or the velocity at which you can throw a softball.

Overall Phase Volume. This is the relative training volume within a given phase compared to the training volume in other training phases throughout the year. Such terms as high, moderate, low, moderately high, or moderately low would be applicable to overall phase volume.

Overall Phase Intensity. Similar to overall phase volume. Overall phase intensity refers to the relative intensity of a particular training phase compared to other training phases throughout the year. Once again, very high, high, moderate, low, moderately high, moderately low, or very low would be appropriate terms to describe intensity.

Figure 8.1

TRAINING PHASE PLANNING GUIDE

Sport/Activity_____

Training Phase _____

Length of Training Phase ____Weeks

Dates of Training Phase _____to_____

Training Goals:

Overall Phase Volume:

Overall Phase Intensity:

___

Weekly Variation of Volume/Intensity

Week 1 _____/_____	Week 5 _____/_____
Week 2 _____/_____	Week 6 _____/_____
Week 3 _____/_____	Week 7 _____/_____
Week 4 _____/_____	Week 8 _____/_____

___

Number of Training Sessions/Week:

Types of Exercises:

Number of Exercises/Training Session:

Set/Repetition Scheme:

Rest Between Sets and Exercises:

Figure 8.1. *Training phase planning guide.*

Weekly Variation of Volume/Intensity. This refers to the volume and intensity of a particular training week within a phase. Even if the overall phase volume is low, somewhere within the training phase the volume will reach a high point. The appropriate term to describe the training volume within this week would be "high" (even though the overall phase volume is low). This is where the concept of relativity kicks in. Similarly, even if the overall phase intensity is high, somewhere within the training phase the intensity must reach a low point (what goes up must come down). Therefore, the appropriate term to describe the weekly intensity would be "low" (even though the overall phase intensity is high). Similar to overall phase volume and overall phase intensity, appropriate terms would be high, moderate, low, moderately high, or moderately low.

Number of Sessions Per Week. Self-explanatory, referring simply to the number of sessions during a particular week of training.

Types of Exercises. Refers to the general types of exercises to be performed during the training phase. Appropriate designations would include multi-joint, single-joint, power type, strength type, or any other term that succinctly describes the basic type of exercises. Other terms that could be used here are one-legged or one-armed, meaning that exercises will be performed using dumbbells or machines on which only one leg or one arm could be trained at a time (also called unilateral training). A term such as plyometric would also be appropriate here.

Number of Exercises per Training Session. Simply refers to the number of exercises to be performed during training sessions within the designated phase. A normal exercise range would be 8-12 exercises per training session. When deciding upon the number of exercises per training session, the total volume of training must be considered. For example, it would be disingenuous to say that during a low-volume training phase there will be 15 exercises per session—unless each exercise was being limited to only one set.

Set Repetition Scheme. This refers to the number of sets and number of repetitions per set to be performed during the training phase. Normally, a range is given for the number of sets and reps per set. Example: the number of sets might range between three and five per exercise and the number of repetitions between eight and ten per set. Naturally, the overall phase volume and intensity must be considered when deciding upon the set repetition scheme. It would be rather contradictory, say, for the overall phase volume to be designated as high and the decision made to perform only one or two sets of each exercise. It would also be difficult to have an overall phase intensity that is high if you make the decision to perform 20 repetitions per set. In order to perform 20 repetitions per set, the resistance used would have to be relatively light, and therefore the intensity would accurately be described as low.

Rest Between Sets and Exercises. Refers to the amount of time allowed for recovery between sets and exercises. Normally, a range is given, such as two to three minutes. This decision must be made considering the overall goals of the training phase. It would be difficult to have a training goal of maximizing 1 RM strength and then decide to have 30-second rest periods between sets and exercises. Such brief rest periods would be inappropriate, because they would not allow sufficient recovery times between lifting the heavy weight. Such heavy resistances are necessary in order to maximize 1 RM strength. After these decisions are made for each training phase, the set/rep range can be filled in on the yearly training plan (Figures 8.2, 8.9, 8.15)

PLAN FOR A STRENGTH/POWER SPORT

A one-year periodization plan for a strength/power sport was developed in Figure 7.2 and is presented again in Figure 8.2. Further development of each training phase is still needed and use of the form presented in Figure 8.1 will help in this process. There are 11 training phases in the yearly periodization plan for a strength/power sport (Figure 8.2). However, there are only six types of training phases within the yearly training plan: recovery, hypertrophy, strength, power, peaking, and competition. Although slight differences will exist between the phase type at various points in the year, in general they will be very similar. For example, a hypertrophy phase, no matter where it is in the year, will have as its major goal an increase in lean body mass or muscle size. Thus, the training plans for the hypertrophy phases will be very similar. Therefore, a general training plan for each type of phase will now be developed.

Figure 8.2

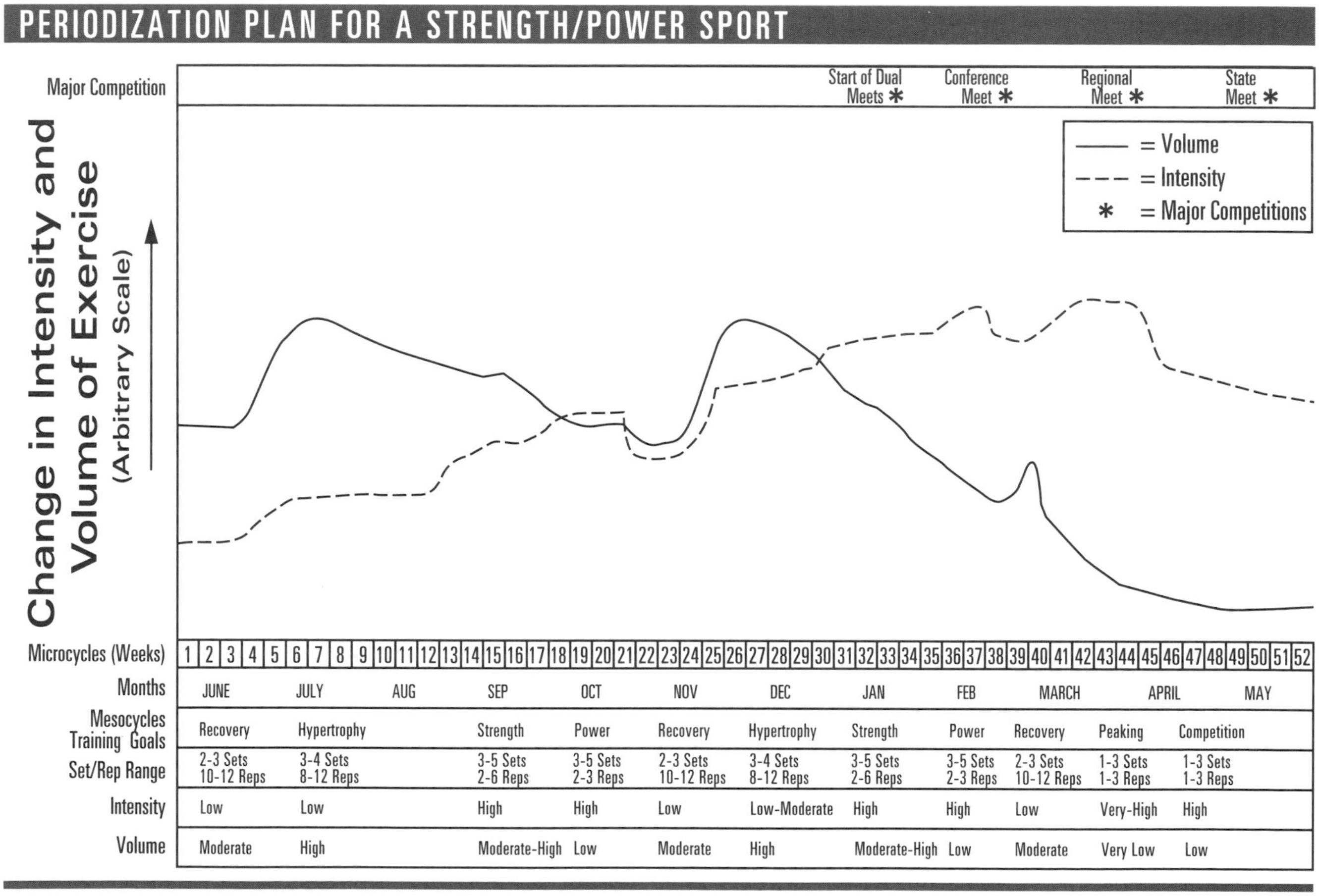

PERIODIZATION PLAN FOR A STRENGTH/POWER SPORT

Figure 8.2. Periodization plan for a strength/power sport.

The initial training phase in the yearly plan for a strength/power sport is a recovery period (Figure 8.3). There are two other short recovery periods evenly spaced throughout the training year. The initial recovery period is four weeks in length, while the other two periods are two weeks in length. Figure 8.3 describes the initial four-week recovery period in June. The goal of all the recovery periods is to allow the athlete to rest up from the previous training phase and prepare their body for the next training phase. All the recovery periods are comprised of moderate volume and low-intensity training. There is little weekly variation in either volume or intensity in any of the recovery periods.

In order to meet the requirements of a moderate volume and low-intensity training period, two to three training sessions are performed per week with only one exercise for each of the major muscle groups. Thus, only 8-10 exercises would be performed per training session. Each exercise is done for two to three sets of 10-12 repetitions per set. Rest periods between sets and exercises are two to three minutes. This combination of number of training sessions per week; type of exercises performed; number of exercises per training session; set repetition scheme; and rest between sets and exercises, will yield the moderate volume and low-intensity training period desired.

Figure 8.4 outlines an eight-week hypertrophy period starting in July. Little change would be necessary in order to describe, say, the six-week hypertrophy period starting in November. The goal of any hypertrophy phase is to increase muscle size and strength. In order to meet this goal, the overall phase volume is relatively high and the overall phase intensity relatively low. There is some weekly variation of volume and intensity in the hypertrophy training phases. As the hypertrophy phase progresses, the volume decreases from high to moderate and the intensity increases from low to moderate and ends with one week of high-intensity training.

To increase the overall training phase volume as compared to the recovery phase volume, three to four training sessions per week are designated, as compared to two to three training sessions per week in the recovery phase. In addition, to increase the training volume over that of the recovery phase, 8-12 exercises are performed per session. The set repetition scheme also results in an increase in volume when compared to the recovery phase: three to five sets per exercise are performed for 8-15 repetitions per set. However, the repetition scheme for multi-joint exercises such as the squat and bench press is different from the set repetition scheme for single-joint exercises such as knee extensions. Eight to twelve repetitions per set are performed for multi-joint exercises; while 10-15 repetitions per set are performed for the single-joint exercises; and 20 repetitions per set performed for abdominal and assistive lower back exercises such as back extensions.

Exercises chosen include at least one for each of the major muscle groups, comprised of both multi-joint and single-joint types. Towards the end of the hypertrophy phase, several power type exercises—such as variations of the snatch, clean, jerk, and certain plyometric type exercises—can be incorporated into the training session. This is done, in part, to inculcate good technique in these exercises, and in part to start to develop the power necessary to be successful in a power type activity such as shot-putting or discus throwing.

The rest between sets and exercises is initially two to three minutes; but is decreased from one to one-and-a-half minutes for single-joint exercises; and held throughout the phase at two to three minutes for multi-joint exercises. This is to allow sufficient recovery between multi-joint sets and exercises so that heavy resistances can be consistently handled. The combination of training variables should result in an increase in muscle size and some increase in muscle strength.

There are two four-week strength phases within the yearly periodization plan (Figure 8.5). As with other phase types, as the training year progresses, the relative intensity later in the year is higher as compared to the same phase earlier in the year. Thus, the first strength phase, occurring in September, is really at a lower intensity than the second strength phase, occurring in June. This is due in large part to the fact that it is anticipated the athlete will be stronger in January than in September. Therefore, the weight used for a given number of repetitions will be higher in the second strength phase as compared to the first strength phase, no matter what the exercise. The result is higher intensity.

The goal of any strength phase is not only to increase strength but, to some extent, muscle size as well. To accomplish this, the overall phase volume is medium to high and the overall phase intensity is high. There is some weekly variation in volume and intensity, with the initial week comprised of high volume and moderate-to-high intensity, while the fourth week is composed of moderate volume and low intensity. As in the hypertrophy phase, there are three to four training sessions per week. Exercise types are mostly multi-joint, with a few single-joint exercises. The number of power type exercises is increased compared to the hypertrophy phase, especially during the last two weeks of the strength phase.

The number of exercises per training session and the set repetition scheme of the strength phase results in a lower overall volume and higher overall intensity as opposed to the hypertrophy stage. Six to ten exercises per training session are performed. There are three to five sets per exercise, but the number of repetitions per set is two to six for the multi-joint exercises and six to ten for the single-joint exercises. The rest between sets and exercises is three to four minutes for multi-joint and two to three minutes for single-joint. The longer rest periods between multi-joint exercises should allow sufficient recovery in order to allow the use of heavy resistances. Although the rest period between sets and exercises for single-joint exercises is shorter than that for multi-joint exercises, it should still be of sufficient length in order to allow the use of relatively heavy resistances during the performance of single-joint exercises.

There are two power phases, each four weeks in length, in the yearly periodization plan for a strength/power sport. Figure 8.6 describes, in general, the training volume and intensity for either of these two power phases. The goal of a power phase is, obviously, to increase power and strength. To accomplish this goal, the overall phase volume is low and the overall phase intensity high. There is some weekly variation of volume and intensity throughout the phase. Generally speaking, as the phase progresses, the training volume decreases and the training intensity increases. There are three training sessions per week. Most multi-joint sporting activities require the development of power. This would include jumping, throwing, and running. It follows that mostly multi-joint power type exercises are used in this phase. The emphasis is on accelerating the weight throughout the entire range of motion of the lifting phase of every exercise (where this can be done safely).

In order to create an overall volume that's lower and an overall phase intensity that's higher than in the strength phase, there are six to eight exercises per training session. The set repetition scheme also results in decreased training volume and increased training intensity. There are three to five sets per exercise, with only two to three repetitions per set for multi-joint and power-type exercises, and six to eight repetitions per set for single-joint exercises. Rest between sets and exercises is three to four minutes for all exercises. This length should allow sufficient recovery so the athlete can use heavy resistances for the small number of repetitions to develop ncar-maximal power with each rep.

The peaking phase in this yearly periodization plan occurs during the dual meet season, right before the major meets, as outlined in Figure 8.7. The peaking phase is six weeks long, and seeks to increase peak power and maintain or increase maximal strength. To accomplish this, the overall phase volume is low to very low and the overall phase intensity high to very high. The weekly variation progresses from moderate to low volume and high intensity during week one, to very low volume and very high intensity during week six. Training volume is kept low and the intensity high by engaging in only two to three training sessions per week, with only four to six exercises per session.

All the exercises performed during this training phase are multi-joint power or multi-joint strength type exercises. The set repetition scheme is one to three sets per exercise and one to three repetitions per set except for abdominal and assistive lower back exercises. The rest between sets and exercises is three to five minutes, which should allow sufficient recovery between all sets and exercises in order to use near-maximal resistances for the desired number of reps.

The competition phase starts prior to the conference meet and stops at the state meet (as outlined in Figure 8.8). The goal of the competition phase is to maintain peak power and strength for all the major competitions of the season. In order to facilitate these goals, the overall phase volume is low and the overall phase intensity high. Little weekly variation in volume or intensity occurs during the competitive phase, with all training sessions composed of low volume and high or very high-intensity training. The highest intensity training during this phase would be performed two weeks prior to the state meet, to afford sufficient recovery time for optimal performance.

The number of training sessions per week is one to three. All exercises are of the multi-joint power or multi-joint strength type. The number of exercises per training session is only three to four, with just one to three sets per exercise, and one to three repetitions per set. The exceptions to the rule here would be abdominal exercises and assistive lower back exercises. The training is truly low volume and high intensity in nature. The rest between sets and exercises is three to five minutes, allowing sufficient recovery for the use of near-maximal resistances in the multi-joint strength exercises, and allowing for near-maximal power to be developed during power type exercises.

STRENGTH/POWER RECOVERY PHASE

Sport/Activity Strength/Power

Training Phase Recovery

Length of Training Phase __4__ **Weeks**

Dates of Training Phase June 1 _____ **to** June 30 _____

Training Goals: Recover from competitive phase, maintain strength, prepare for hypertrophy phase.

Overall Phase Volume: Moderate.

Overall Phase Intensity: Low

Weekly Variation of Volume/Intensity

Week 1 __Moderate__ / __Low__   **Week 5** _____ / _____

Week 2 __Moderate__ / __Low__   **Week 6** _____ / _____

Week 3 __Moderate__ / __Low__   **Week 7** _____ / _____

Week 4 __Moderate__ / __Low__   **Week 8** _____ / _____

Number of Training Sessions/Week: 2-3.

Types of Exercises: One for each major muscle group.

Number of Exercises/Training Session: 8-10

Set/Repetition Scheme: 2-3 sets/exercise, 10-12 reps/set.

Rest Between Sets and Exercises: 2-3 minutes.

Figure 8.3. Strength/power recovery phase.

Figure 8.4

STRENGTH/POWER HYPERTROPHY PHASE

Sport/Activity Strength/Power

Training Phase Hypertrophy

Length of Training Phase _8_ **Weeks**

Dates of Training Phase July 1 **to** August 31

Training Goals: Increase muscle size and strength.

Overall Phase Volume: High.

Overall Phase Intensity: Low.

Weekly Variation of Volume/Intensity

Week 1 High / Low		**Week 5** Moderate-High / Moderate
Week 2 High / Low		**Week 6** Moderate-High / Moderate
Week 3 High / Low		**Week 7** Moderate-High / Moderate
Week 4 Moderate / Low		**Week 8** Moderate / High

Number of Training Sessions/Week: 3-4.

Types of Exercises: At least one for each major muscle group, multiple joint and single joint will be used, few power type exercises.

Number of Exercises/Training Session: 8-12.

Set/Repetition Scheme: 3-5 sets/exercise, 8-12 reps/set for multi-joint exercises, 10-15 for single-joint exercises, 20 reps/set for abdominal and assistive lower back exercises.

Rest Between Sets and Exercises: Initially 2-3 minutes, decreasing to 1-1.5 minutes at end of phase for single-joint exercises.

Figure 8.4. Strength/power hypertrophy phase.

Figure 8.5

STRENGTH/POWER STRENGTH PHASE

Sport/Activity Strength/Power

Training Phase Strength

Length of Training Phase 4 **Weeks**

Dates of Training Phase September 1 **to** September 30

Training Goals: Increase strength, some increase in muscle size.

Overall Phase Volume: Medium-High.

Overall Phase Intensity: High.

Weekly Variation of Volume/Intensity

Week 1 High / Moderate-High	**Week 5** /
Week 2 High / High	**Week 6** /
Week 3 Moderate-High / High	**Week 7** /
Week 4 Moderate / Low	**Week 8** /

Number of Training Sessions/Week: 3-4.

Types of Exercises: Mostly multi-joint, some power type exercises especially in last 2 weeks of phase.

Number of Exercises/Training Session: 6-10.

Set/Repetition Scheme: 3-5 sets/exercise, 2-6 reps/set for multi-joint exercises, 6-10 for single-joint exercises, 20 reps/set for abdominals and assistive lower back exercises.

Rest Between Sets and Exercises: 3-4 minutes for multi-joint exercises, 2-3 minutes for single-joint exercises.

Figure 8.5. Strength/power strength phase.

Figure 8.6

STRENGTH/POWER POWER PHASE

Sport/Activity Strength/Power

Training Phase Power

Length of Training Phase 4 **Weeks**

Dates of Training Phase October 1 **to** October 31

Training Goals: Increase power, increase strength.

Overall Phase Volume: Low.

Overall Phase Intensity: High.

Weekly Variation of Volume/Intensity

Week 1 Moderate-Low / Moderate-High   **Week 5** _____ / _____

Week 2 Moderate-Low / High   **Week 6** _____ / _____

Week 3 Low / High   **Week 7** _____ / _____

Week 4 Low / High   **Week 8** _____ / _____

Number of Training Sessions/Week: 3.

Types of Exercises: Mostly multi-joint, mostly power type exercises, emphasis on accelerating weight during all sets.

Number of Exercises/Training Session: 6-8.

Set/Repetition Scheme: 3-5 sets/exercise, 2-3 reps/set for multi-joint and power exercises, 6-8 reps/set for single-joint exercises, 20 reps/set for abdominals and assistive lower back exercises.

Rest Between Sets and Exercises: 3-4 minutes for all exercises.

Figure 8.6. Strength/power power phase.

Figure 8.7

STRENGTH/POWER PEAKING PHASE

Sport/Activity Strength/Power

Training Phase Peaking

Length of Training Phase 6 **Weeks**

Dates of Training Phase February 1 **to** April 13

Training Goals: Increase peak power, and maintain or increase strength.

Overall Phase Volume: Low-Very Low.

Overall Phase Intensity: High-Very High.

Weekly Variation of Volume/Intensity

Week 1 Moderate-Low / High	**Week 5** Very Low / Very High
Week 2 Low / High	**Week 6** Very Low / Very High
Week 3 Low / High	**Week 7** /
Week 4 Very Low / High	**Week 8** /

Number of Training Sessions/Week: 2-3.

Types of Exercises: Multi-joint power, multi-joint strength.

Number of Exercises/Training Session: 4-6.

Set/Repetition Scheme: 1-3 sets/exercise, 1-3 reps/set except for abdominal and assistive lower back exercises.

Rest Between Sets and Exercises: 3-5 minutes.

Figure 8.7. Strength/power peaking phase.

Figure 8.8

STRENGTH/POWER COMPETITIVE PHASE

Sport/Activity Strength/Power

Training Phase Competition

Length of Training Phase 8 **Weeks**

Dates of Training Phase April 14 **to** May 29

Training Goals: Maintain peak power and strength.

Overall Phase Volume: Low.

Overall Phase Intensity: High.

Weekly Variation of Volume/Intensity

Week 1 Low / High   **Week 5** Low / High

Week 2 Low / High   **Week 6** Low / Very High

Week 3 Low / High   **Week 7** Low / High

Week 4 Low / High   **Week 8** Low / High

Number of Training Sessions/Week: 1-3.

Types of Exercises: Multi-joint power, multi-joint strength.

Number of Exercises/Training Session: 3-4.

Set/Repetition Scheme: 1-3 sets/exercise, 1-3 reps/set except for abdominal exercises and assistive lower back exercises.

Rest Between Sets and Exercises: 3-5 minutes.

Figure 8.8. Strength/power competitive phase.

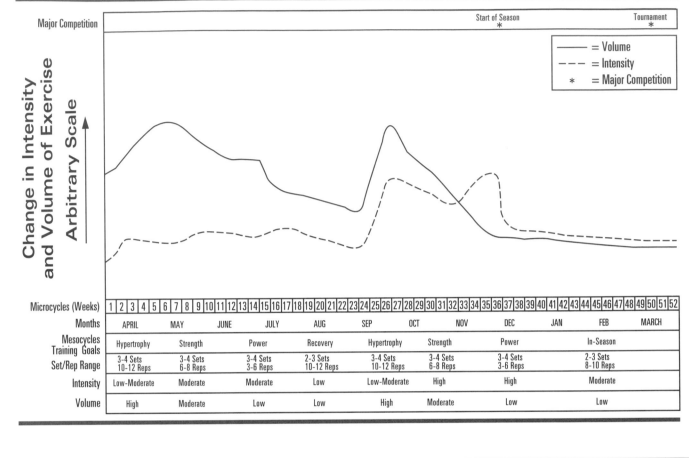

PERIODIZATION PLAN FOR BASKETBALL

Microcycles (Weeks)	1 2 3 4 5 6 7 8 9 10 11 12 13 14 15 16 17 18 19 20 21 22 23 24 25 26 27 28 29 30 31 32 33 34 35 36 37 38 39 40 41 42 43 44 45 46 47 48 49 50 51 52							
Months	APRIL	MAY	JUNE	JULY	AUG	SEP	OCT	NOV	DEC	JAN	FEB	MARCH
Mesocycles Training Goals	Hypertrophy	Strength	Power	Recovery	Hypertrophy	Strength	Power	In-Season
Set/Rep Range	3-4 Sets 10-12 Reps	3-4 Sets 6-8 Reps	3-4 Sets 3-6 Reps	2-3 Sets 10-12 Reps	3-4 Sets 10-12 Reps	3-4 Sets 6-8 Reps	3-4 Sets 3-6 Reps	2-3 Sets 8-10 Reps
Intensity	Low-Moderate	Moderate	Moderate	Low	Low-Moderate	High	High	Moderate
Volume	High	Moderate	Low	Low	High	Moderate	Low	Low

Figure 8.9. Periodization Plan for Basketball

PLAN FOR BASKETBALL

A yearly periodized strength training plan for basketball was developed in Figure 7.3, and can now be seen again in Figure 8.9. Each training phase or macrocycle will now be further developed. This periodization plan for basketball will take its cue from the training phase guiding plan (Figure 8.1). There are five types of training phases within the yearly plan for basketball.

The training year begins with an eight-week hypertrophy phase starting in April. Figure 8.10 describes, in more detail, the weight training undertaken during this hypertrophy phase. With little alteration, Figure 8.10 could also be used to describe the eight-week hypertrophy phase beginning in September. The goal of the hypertrophy phase is to increase muscle size and overall muscular strength.

The overall phase volume is high and the overall phase intensity low to moderate during the hypertrophy phase. In week one, volume is moderate and intensity low.

During weeks two through seven, volume and intensity are gradually increased. In week seven, both volume and intensity reach a high point for the training phase. During week eight, volume is decreased to a moderate-high level and intensity to a moderate level. This is to allow some recovery prior to the initiation of the subsequent strength phase. The number of training sessions per week is three throughout the phase.

In order to keep the training volume relatively high, there are 8-12 exercises per training session with three or four sets of 10-12 repetitions per set, except for lower back assistive and abdominal exercises. Sets consist of multi-joint and single-joint exercises, with at least one exercise for all the major muscle groups of the body. The rest between sets and exercises is initially three minutes, with a gradual decrease to one minute by week eight of the hypertrophy phase.

Each strength phase within the training year is six weeks in length (Figure 8.11). The major goal is to increase overall body strength. Both overall phase volume and overall phase intensity are at a moderate level during the strength phases. During week one, training volume is at its high point for the phase, and is then maintained at the moderate level for the remaining weeks. Intensity during week one is at a moderate level, then progresses to a high level during weeks four and five, and is reduced to the moderate level during week six. The decrease in intensity during week six should allow for some recovery prior to the beginning of the power phase.

There are three training sessions per week. Exercises are predominantly of the multi-joint strength type, such as the squat, bench press, leg press, and military press. Some single-joint exercises are also included in each training session. In order to decrease overall phase volume and increase overall phase intensity, as compared to the hypertrophy phase, there are only eight to ten exercises per training session. But similar to the hypertrophy phase, we concentrate on three to four sets of each exercise, although the number of repetitions per set is decreased to six to eight. Two to three minutes rest are allowed between sets and exercises, allowing sufficient recovery from the use of heavy resistances during each set.

Both of the power phases are four weeks in length (Figure 8.12). The major goal of each is to increase overall body power so that sport-specific skills like vertical jump ability increase. Overall phase volume is low and overall phase intensity moderate. Weekly training volume is at its high point during week one, followed by two weeks in which training volume is moderate, and then low during week four. With the lowest training volume and a moderate intensity during week four, some recovery time should transpire before you begin the next phase.

The number of training sessions per week is three. Exercise types are predominately multi-joint power exercises, such as variations of the snatch, jumps with dumbbells, and plyometric type exercises. In addition, some multi-joint strength exercises such as the leg press and bench press will be performed in order to maintain the overall body strength developed during the hypertrophy and strength phases. In order to have an overall phase volume that is low and an overall phase intensity that's moderate, the number of exercises per training session is six to ten, three to four sets, three to six repetitions per set. The rest between sets and exercises is initially three minutes, increasing to four minutes by the end of the phase. It's increased as the phase progresses so that sufficient recovery occurs to allow for development of near-maximal power during each set.

The recovery phase is two weeks in length (Figure 8.13). After the completion of the first hypertrophy strength and power phase, a short recovery period is necessary to allow both physical and psychological recovery, and to prepare for the upcoming training phase. Overall phase volume and overall phase intensity are low in order to facilitate the process. They are kept low by performing two to three training sessions per week, with two to three sets per exercise, 10-12 repetitions per set. In order to prevent deconditioning during the recovery phase, there is at least one exercise for all the major muscle groups during each training session. The recovery phase should result in maintenance of strength and power gains achieved during the preceding training phases, and allow for physiological/psychological recovery in preparation for the next training phase.

The in-season program is 14 weeks (Figure 8.14). The goal of the in-season program is to maintain all the gains made during the previous training phases and to prevent injury in competition circumstances. Overall phase volume is low and overall phase intensity moderate. This is necessary so that sufficient training time can be dedicated to the development and maintenance of basketball-specific skills. Low training volume and moderate training intensity are also necessary so that the overall training load—including playing several games a week, basketball specific drills, physical conditioning other than weight training, and weight training—does not result in over-training.

Several variations have been built into the in-season training program in order to keep the phase volume low and intensity moderate. The number of training sessions per week will vary between one and three, depending upon the playing schedule. Exercises will all be multi-joint in nature. This will reduce the total amount of training time that must be dedicated to weight training, thus allowing more time to be devoted to the development of basketball-specific skills and strategies.

The number of exercises per training session ranges from four to eight, with two to three sets of each exercise, and 8-10 repetitions per set. The rest period between sets and exercises is two minutes.

Figure 8.10

BASKETBALL HYPERTROPHY PHASE

Sport/Activity Basketball

Training Phase Hypertrophy

Length of Training Phase 8 **Weeks**

Dates of Training Phase April 1 **to** May 23

Training Goals: Increase muscle size, increase overall strength.

Overall Phase Volume: High.

Overall Phase Intensity: Low-Moderate.

Weekly Variation of Volume/Intensity

Week 1	Moderate / Low	**Week 5**	High / Moderate
Week 2	Moderate / Low	**Week 6**	High / Moderate
Week 3	Moderate-High / Moderate	**Week 7**	High / High
Week 4	Moderate-High / Moderate	**Week 8**	Moderate-High / Moderate

Number of Training Sessions/Week: 3.

Types of Exercises: Multi-joint and single-joint, at least one exercise for each major muscle group.

Number of Exercises/Training Session: 8-12.

Set/Repetition Scheme: 3-4 sets/exercise, 10-12 reps/set except for lower back assistive and abdominals where up to 25 reps/set will be performed.

Rest Between Sets and Exercises: Initially 3 minutes decreasing to 1 by end of phase.

Figure 8.10. Basketball hypertrophy phase.

Figure 8.11

BASKETBALL STRENGTH PHASE

Sport/Activity Basketball

Training Phase Strength

Length of Training Phase 6 **Weeks**

Dates of Training Phase May 24 **to** July 4

Training Goals: Increase total body strength.

Overall Phase Volume: Moderate.

Overall Phase Intensity: Moderate.

Weekly Variation of Volume/Intensity

Week 1 High / Moderate	**Week 5** Moderate / High
Week 2 Moderate / Moderate	**Week 6** Moderate-High / Moderate
Week 3 Moderate-Low / Moderate-High	**Week 7** /
Week 4 Moderate / High	**Week 8** /

Number of Training Sessions/Week: 3.

Types of Exercises: Multi-joint and single-joint, at least one exercise for each major muscle group.

Number of Exercises/Training Session: 8-10.

Set/Repetition Scheme: 3-4 sets/exercise, 6-8 reps/set except abdominals.

Rest Between Sets and Exercises: 2-3 minutes.

Figure 8.11. Basketball strength phase.

Figure 8.12

BASKETBALL POWER PHASE

Sport/Activity Basketball

Training Phase Power

Length of Training Phase 4 **Weeks**

Dates of Training Phase July 5 **to** August 1

Training Goals: Increase power, maintain strength.

Overall Phase Volume: Low.

Overall Phase Intensity: Moderate.

Weekly Variation of Volume/Intensity

Week 1 High / Low   **Week 5** _____ / _____

Week 2 Moderate / High   **Week 6** _____ / _____

Week 3 Moderate / High   **Week 7** _____ / _____

Week 4 Low / Moderate   **Week 8** _____ / _____

Number of Training Sessions/Week: 3.

Types of Exercises: Multi-joint, power and strength.

Number of Exercises/Training Session: 6-10.

Set/Repetition Scheme: 3-4 sets/exercise, 3-6 reps/set except abdominals.

Rest Between Sets and Exercises: Initially 3 minutes increasing to 4 minutes by end of phase.

Figure 8.12. Basketball power phase.

Figure 8.13

BASKETBALL RECOVERY PHASE

Sport/Activity Basketball

Training Phase Recovery

Length of Training Phase 2 **Weeks**

Dates of Training Phase August 2 **to** August 15

Training Goals: Recover from previous training, but maintain strength and power gains.

Overall Phase Volume: Low.

Overall Phase Intensity: Low.

Weekly Variation of Volume/Intensity

Week 1 High / High   **Week 5** _____ / _____

Week 2 Low / Low   **Week 6** _____ / _____

Week 3 _____ / _____   **Week 7** _____ / _____

Week 4 _____ / _____   **Week 8** _____ / _____

Number of Training Sessions/Week: 2-3.

Types of Exercises: Multi-joint strength, single joint, at least one exercise for each major muscle group.

Number of Exercises/Training Session: 8-10.

Set/Repetition Scheme: 2-3 sets/exercise, 10-12 reps/set except for abdominals.

Rest Between Sets and Exercises: 2-3 minutes.

Figure 8.13. Basketball recovery phase.

Figure 8.14

BASKETBALL IN-SEASON PHASE

Sport/Activity Basketball

Training Phase In-Season

Length of Training Phase ____**Weeks**

Dates of Training Phase December 15 **to** March 30

Training Goals: Maintain gains made during the previous training phases.

Overall Phase Volume: Low.

Overall Phase Intensity: Moderate.

Weekly Variation of Volume/Intensity

Week 1	Low	/ Moderate	**Week 5**		/
Week 2	Low	/ Moderate	**Week 6**		/
Week 3	Low	/ Moderate	**Week 7**		/
Week 4	Low	/ Moderate	**Week 8**		/

Number of Training Sessions/Week: 1-3 depending upon game schedule.

Types of Exercises: Multi-joint.

Number of Exercises/Training Session: 4-8.

Set/Repetition Scheme: 2-3 sets/exercise, 8-10 reps/set, except abdominals.

Rest Between Sets and Exercises: 2 minutes.

Figure 8.14. Basketball in-season phase.

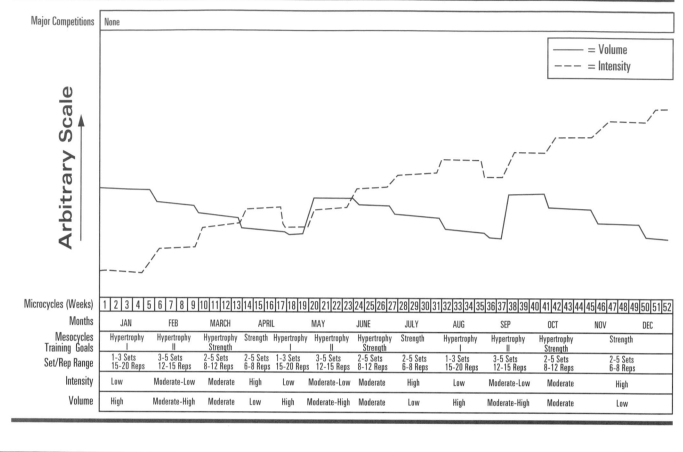

Figure 8.15. *Periodization plan for general fitness.*

P E R I O D I Z A T I O N   P L A N
F O R   G E N E R A L   F I T N E S S

A year-long periodization plan for general fitness was developed in Figure 7.4 and is reintroduced in Figure 8.15.

There are three hypertrophy I (as opposed to hypertrophy II) training phases within the year, each four weeks in length. The training plan for each of the hypertrophy I training phases is further developed in Figure 8.16. The goal of the hypertrophy I phase is to increase muscle size and strength. The overall phase volume is high and overall phase intensity is low. No weekly variation in volume and intensity is included in the plan. However, the weight used for any particular exercise should be increasing as the phase progresses. Therefore, intensity will be gradually but consistently increased. The number of training sessions during week one is two, but should then be increased to three sessions during week two or three. This is to allow time for the trainee to become accustomed to the stress of resistance training.

At least one exercise for all major muscle groups—of a multi-joint or a single-joint type—should be included in each training session, 8-12 exercises in all. Again to allow time for the trainee to become accustomed to resistance training during week one, only one set of each exercise might be performed; in week two, two sets might be performed; and during weeks three and four, three sets. Although little variation in intensity is planned, it is possible to increase the intensity slightly throughout the training phase by initially performing 20 repetitions per set during week one, then progressing to 15 repetitions (which means a heavier resistance) per set by the fourth week.

Rest between sets and exercises is initially three minutes, decreasing to one or two minutes during the fourth week. Longer rest periods at the start of the training phase should allow sufficient recovery so that the trainee can tolerate the stress. It is also possible to rest two minutes between sets, but only one minute between exercises. With the trainee accustomed to resistance training, and the rest periods decreased, the result should be a greater stimulus for hypertrophy. For men and women on a tight time schedule, decreasing the total amount of time necessary for a training session is an important consideration. The hypertrophy I training phases, as outlined, should result in an increase in muscle size and strength, and prepare the trainee for the subsequent training phases.

The hypertrophy II training phases are outlined in Figure 8.17. Similar in nature to the hypertrophy I phases, the goal of hypertrophy II phases is to increase muscle size and strength. The overall phase volume is moderate to high and overall phase intensity moderate to low. Each of the hypertrophy II training phases is four weeks in length. In common with the hypertrophy I phases, little weekly variation in volume and intensity is planned.

The hypertrophy I phase should have prepared the trainee for three sessions per week. Again in accordance with the hypertrophy I phase, there are 8-12 exercises per training session. Each training session should include multi-joint and single-joint type exercises, with at least one exercise for each major muscle group.

In order to increase the intensity of training (compared to the hypertrophy I phase), there are 12-15 reps per set with, in general, three sets per exercise. However, you can do four to five sets of an exercise if the desire is to emphasize a particular body part. It's also possible to add another exercise for a body part you're looking to emphasize, instead of performing more sets of the same exercise. For example, instead of performing five sets of standing calf raises, three sets of standing calf raises and two sets of donkey calf raises could be substituted. This allows variation in the training plan to meet the needs and goals of a trainee—which, lest we forget, is what periodization is all about.

Rest periods between sets and exercises should be one to two minutes. To add training variation, it's possible to plan for two-minute rest periods during week one, decreasing the length to one minute as the trainee becomes accustomed to training stress. Again, the amount of rest between sets can be different than the amount between exercises. The hypertrophy II phase should show a nice increase in muscle size and strength.

The hypertrophy/strength training phase is outlined in Figure 8.18. The emphasis here is slightly more on strength than hypertrophy. The overall phase volume and intensity are both moderate. As with both the hypertrophy phases, little weekly variation in volume and intensity is planned. The number of training sessions per week is three. The overall phase volume is decreased slightly and the overall phase intensity increased slightly compared to the hypertrophy II phase, with 8-10 exercises per training session, two to five sets per exercise, and 8-12 repetitions per set. Exercises are mostly of the multi-joint type, although some single-joint exercises can be included if desired. The rest between sets and exercises is one to two minutes.

Since this phase emphasizes strength slightly more than hypertrophy, it may be desirable to initially take a one-minute rest period during week one and, as the training phase progresses, gradually lengthening this period to two minutes by week four. By allowing more recovery time, trainees can use a greater amount of resistance for the desired number of sets and reps. The two-minute rest period should ostensibly allow greater strength development.

Each strength phase is four weeks in length, and is further delineated in Figure 8.19. The major goal of the strength phase is to increase overall body strength and maintain muscle size. It is in this phase that overall intensity reaches its high point and overall phase volume reaches its low point. Similar to all of the preceding phases, little variation in weekly volume and intensity is planned. However, as in all the other phases, as the individual becomes stronger, the weight used for the desired number of repetitions and sets should increase, leading to an inevitable increase in intensity throughout training. There are three training sessions per week, using mostly multi-joint exercises.

An increase in overall intensity and a decrease in overall volume as compared to the other training phases is facilitated by performing only six to eight exercises per training session. In addition, the higher intensity and lower volume training is made possible by choosing to perform only six to eight repetitions per set. This allows the use of the heaviest weights within the entire year's program.

Choosing to do two to five sets of an exercise per training session allows the individual to tailor the regimen to meet their needs. If the trainee prefers to emphasize maximal strength development in one or two exercises such as the bench press and squat, then they might want to emphasize these heavy-duty exercises by going for five sets, and doing as few as two sets of other exercises less optimally related to their strength training goals.

Rest between sets and exercises ranges from between two to four minutes. Longer rest periods are preferable if the individual truly wishes to emphasize maximal strength development. One thing is clear: following this general fitness program will result in palpable gains in total body strength.

Figure 8.16

GENERAL FITNESS HYPERTROPHY I PHASE

Sport/Activity _General Fitness_

Training Phase _Hypertrophy I_

Length of Training Phase _4_ **Weeks**

Dates of Training Phase _January 1_ **to** _January 31_

Training Goals: Increase muscle size, increase strength.

Overall Phase Volume: High.

Overall Phase Intensity: Low.

Weekly Variation of Volume/Intensity

Week 1	_High_	/ _Low_	**Week 5**		/
Week 2	_High_	/ _Low_	**Week 6**		/
Week 3	_High_	/ _Low_	**Week 7**		/
Week 4	_High_	/ _Low_	**Week 8**		/

Number of Training Sessions/Week: 2-3. Week 1, 2 sessions progressing to 3 in week 2 or 3.

Types of Exercises: Multi-joint and single-joint, at least one for each major muscle group.

Number of Exercises/Training Session: 8-12.

Set/Repetition Scheme: 1-3 sets/exercise, 15-20 reps/set, initially 20 reps/set decreasing to 15 reps/set in fourth week.

Rest Between Sets and Exercises: 1-3 minutes, initially 3 minutes decreasing to 1 or 2 during fourth week.

Figure 8.16. *General fitness hypertrophy I phase.*

Figure 8.17

GENERAL FITNESS HYPERTROPHY II PHASE

Sport/Activity General Fitness

Training Phase Hypertrophy II

Length of Training Phase 4 **Weeks**

Dates of Training Phase February 1 **to** February 28

Training Goals: Increase muscle size and strength.

Overall Phase Volume: Moderate-High.

Overall Phase Intensity: Moderate-Low.

Weekly Variation of Volume/Intensity

Week 1 Moderate-High / Moderate-Low	**Week 5** ___ / ___
Week 2 Moderate-High / Moderate-Low	**Week 6** ___ / ___
Week 3 Moderate-High / Moderate-Low	**Week 7** ___ / ___
Week 4 Moderate-High / Moderate-Low	**Week 8** ___ / ___

Number of Training Sessions/Week: 3.

Types of Exercises: Multi-joint and single-joint, at least one for each major muscle group.

Number of Exercises/Training Session: 8-12.

Set/Repetition Scheme: 3-5 sets/exercise, 12-15 reps/set, use 4-5 sets for body parts needing emphasis.

Rest Between Sets and Exercises: 1-2 minutes.

Figure 8.17. General fitness hypertrophy II phase.

Figure 8.18

GENERAL FITNESS HYPERTROPHY/STRENGTH PHASE

Sport/Activity General Fitness

Training Phase Hypertrophy/Strength

Length of Training Phase 4 **Weeks**

Dates of Training Phase March 1 **to** March 31

Training Goals: Increase strength and hypertrophy.

Overall Phase Volume: Moderate.

Overall Phase Intensity: Moderate.

Weekly Variation of Volume/Intensity

Week 1 Moderate / Moderate   **Week 5** _____/_____

Week 2 Moderate / Moderate   **Week 6** _____/_____

Week 3 Moderate / Moderate   **Week 7** _____/_____

Week 4 Moderate / Moderate   **Week 8** _____/_____

Number of Training Sessions/Week: 3.

Types of Exercises: Mostly multi-joint, some single-joint.

Number of Exercises/Training Session: 8-10.

Set/Repetition Scheme: 2-5 sets/exercise, 8-12 reps/set, except for abdominals.

Rest Between Sets and Exercises: 1-2 minutes.

Figure 8.18. General fitness hypertrophy/strength phase.

Figure 8.19

GENERAL FITNESS STRENGTH PHASE

Sport/Activity General Fitness

Training Phase Strength

Length of Training Phase 4 **Weeks**

Dates of Training Phase April 1 **to** April 30

Training Goals: Increase strength, maintain muscle size.

Overall Phase Volume: Low.

Overall Phase Intensity: High.

Weekly Variation of Volume/Intensity

Week 1 Low / High		**Week 5** /	
Week 2 Low / High		**Week 6** /	
Week 3 Low / High		**Week 7** /	
Week 4 Low / High		**Week 8** /	

Number of Training Sessions/Week: 3.

Types of Exercises: Mostly multi-joint.

Number of Exercises/Training Session: 6-8.

Set/Repetition Scheme: 2-5 sets/exercise, 6-8 reps/set, except for abdominals.

Rest Between Sets and Exercises: 2-4 minutes.

Figure 8.19. General fitness strength phase.

Having expanded upon the details of training phases (mesocycles) in this chapter, in the next chapter we look at planning weeks of training within each phase.

planning a week of training

t he basics for putting together a yearly training plan were discussed in chapter 7. In chapter 8, using the yearly training plan as a guideline, each training phase was further developed. Now, keeping in mind the training phase plans developed in chapter 8, each week of training within a phase will be carefully developed. You'll recall also that the basic foundation material was touched upon in chapter 5 ("Weekly Models of Periodization").

There can be—and inevitably, will be—considerable overlap when developing a yearly, monthly, or weekly training plan. For example, the number of training sessions per week during each training phase of the yearly cycle is planned out when the yearly cycle is first developed. However, when further developing each week of training within a phase, decisions such as whether or not a training session should be heavy, moderate, or light must be made.

Use the form found in Figure 9.1 (Weekly Training Variation). It will greatly help you in the organization and development of each week in a training phase. As the natural progression is made from the yearly to the monthly to the weekly training plan, more and more cogent details are developed.

In general, the number and type of exercises to be in a training session will have already been decided at this point. However, to further develop the weekly training plan, it must now be decided how many multi-joint, single-joint, single limb, arm, leg, abdomen, low back, or power type exercises will be included. While a range for the number of sets and repetitions has also been decided upon, decisions about the number of sets and reps for individual exercises must now be zeroed in on.

Similarly, a range for rest periods between sets and exercises has been determined, but the exact length of rest time will become more clear as you focus in on a weekly basis.

Essentially, planning the weekly training variation is nothing more than expanding upon and fine-tuning the decisions that have already been made. But this is, nonetheless, a very important stage in your periodization plan.

Figure 9.1

WEEKLY TRAINING VARIATION

Sport/Activity _____   Dates of Training Phase _____ to _____

Training Phase _____

	Volume/Intensity	Sessions per Week	Number and Type of Exercises	Set/Rep Scheme	Rest Between Sets and Exercises
Week 1					
Week 2					
Week 3					
Week 4					
Week 5					
Week 6					
Week 7					
Week 8					

Figure 9.1. Weekly training variation.

The yearly training plan for strength/power is shown in Figure 8.2; and each phase of the strength/power periodization plan was delineated in Figures 8.3 to 8.8. Now it's time to focus in on each week of the strength/power periodization plan in order to further develop it.

The strength/power recovery phase is four weeks long and essentially consists of two weeks of relatively light training followed by two weeks of slightly more intense training (Figure 8.3). To make the training slightly more intense during the last two weeks of the phase, several changes in the weekly training variation have been made. During the first two weeks, there are two exercise sessions per week; the last two weeks, there are three training sessions per week (Figure 9.2). In addition, for week one, each of the two training sessions is light in nature; during weeks three and four, the training sessions are alternately heavy, moderate, and light.

The only major change in the number and type of exercises between the first two weeks and the last two weeks is the inclusion of two multi-joint exercises during the first two weeks versus three multi-joint exercises during the last two weeks.

When charting the number and type of exercises, abbreviations can be used. For example, MJ stands for multi-joint exercises such as the squat, bench press, or leg press. MJP stands for multi-joint power exercises such as snatch or clean pulls. "Arm" stands for single-joint arm and shoulder exercises such as arm curls and lateral shoulder raises. "Leg" stands for single-joint leg exercises such as knee curls and calf raises. "Ab" stands for abdominal exercises such as sit-ups or crunches. "Low back" stands for low back exercises like back extensions. There are a multitude of other possible abbreviations—literally whatever shorthand makes sense to you.

The first week of the recovery phase is the lightest, with only two sets of each exercise. During weeks two, three, and four, there are three sets of each exercise. Throughout all four weeks of this phase, there are a consistent 10-12 repetitions per set. The rest between sets and exercises is three minutes during the first two weeks, two minutes during the last two weeks. This makes the entire session slightly more intense during the last two weeks of the phase.

Weekly variations of the hypertrophy training phase are developed from guidelines seen in Figure 8.4. The first three weeks of the phase consist of high volume and relatively low-intensity training; weeks four through seven consist of moderate to high intensity and low-to-moderate volume training; while week eight consists of high-intensity training of moderate volume. Several variables have been manipulated to create changes in volume and intensity (Figure 9.3). During weeks one through three, there's three training sessions per week; weeks four through seven consist of four training sessions per week; and week eight, three training sessions per week. The highest intensity training is performed during weeks six and seven, where two heavy days of training are scheduled.

The total number of exercises per training session remains relatively consistent throughout the phase. However, during week four, one multi-joint power type exercise (MJP)—such as a power clean or power snatch—is incorporated into the training session and remains through week eight. This is done, in part, to initiate the development of power capabilities necessary in a strength power athlete; and to begin to perfect the technique of power-oriented exercises in preparation for subsequent training phases.

The training volume of multi-joint exercises is gradually increased from week one through week seven, then slightly decreased during week eight. The training intensity of multi-joint exercises is increased during the phase by decreasing the number of reps per set from 10 to 8.

The training volume and intensity of single-joint exercises also varies throughout this training phase. This is accomplished by changing the number of sets and the number of repetitions per set of single-joint exercises throughout the training phase. The highest volume of single-joint exercises occurs during weeks three and four when four sets of 15 repetitions are performed. The highest intensity of single-joint exercises is found during week eight when three sets of 10 repetitions per exercise are performed. The manipulation of the multi-joint and single-joint training volume and intensity results in the highest total training volume during weeks three and four and the highest training intensity in weeks seven and eight.

Rest between sets and exercises also changes throughout the training phase. Initially, the rest periods are three minutes in length, gradually decreasing to two minutes for all exercises during weeks four and five. During weeks six and seven, three-minute rest periods are interspersed between multi-joint exercises so the athlete can more completely recover and handle heavier weights. Rest periods for single-joint exercises during weeks six and seven are further decreased to 1.5 minutes to help stimulate muscle growth. During week eight, two-minute rest periods are employed. The decrease in total training volume in week eight (by having three training sessions per week instead of four, and decreasing the number of sets of multi-joint exercises from five to four) should result in some recovery prior to the start of the next strength phase.

A key consideration when looking at the hypertrophy phase is that training variables such as the number of sets, repetitions per set, and rest periods between sets and exercises, can be different for various types of exercises, such as multi-joint versus single-joint.

The strength phase runs four weeks. Originally outlined in Figure 8.5, the weekly variation is further developed in Figure 9.4. Training volume is highest during the first two weeks of the phase and intensity highest during the last two weeks. The goal of this phase is to increase total body strength. Four multi-joint exercises such as squats or bench presses and two multi-joint power exercises such as power cleans or power snatches are included for each training session throughout the phase.

Training volume of multi-joint exercises is highest during weeks two and three, when five sets of each exercise are performed. During week three training intensity for multi-joint exercises (two to five repetitions per set) is slightly higher than during week two (three to six repetitions per set). The intensity of the multi-joint exercises is highest during week four, when only two to three reps per set are performed. Training volume for single-joint exercises is highest during the first week of training (four sets of eight to ten repetitions are performed). During weeks two through four, the volume of single-joint exercises is decreased slightly, compared to week one with only three sets of eight repetitions.

Rest periods between sets and exercises are longer during weeks three and four than during weeks one and two. This is to allow a more complete recovery so that very heavy weights for the desired number of repetitions can be used during the final two weeks, keeping intensity high to increase maximal strength.

It is also important to note the arrangement of heavy, moderate, and light training days throughout the phase. Training is actually more difficult during weeks one, two, and three than during week four, because these weeks contain more heavy and moderate days. Total training volume is decreased slightly during week four, by performing four versus five sets of multi-joint exercises to allow the use of heavy weight and to permit proper recovery between phases.

The four-week power phase was outlined in Figure 8.6 and the weekly variation further developed in Figure 9.5. The effectiveness of power training is, in part, dependent upon adequate recovery between training sessions. Sufficient recovery is necessary so that near-maximal power levels can be developed. Therefore, throughout this phase there are only three training sessions per week. By the same token, sufficient recovery must also be allowed between exercises and sets. Characteristic of the entire phase, three and four-minute rest periods are allowed.

Power training must also be performed at a relatively high intensity to be effective. The weekly pattern of heavy, light, and moderate training days reflects this concept. During week two, one heavy and two moderate training sessions are scheduled; during weeks three and four, it's two heavy and one light training session.

For power training to be truly effective, the total volume of training must be kept low. Low volume is reflected in the relatively small number of exercises per session and the small number of repetitions per set. The use of two to three repetitions per set allows for the use of relatively heavy resistances, which in turn maintains a very high level of intensity.

The power phase immediately precedes the peaking phase. A power training scheme should prepare the athlete to develop maximal strength and power during the peaking phase.

The peaking phase is six weeks in length, as originally outlined in Figure 8.7, with further modifications of weekly variation depicted in Figure 9.6. In order to peak for maximal strength and power, high intensity, low-volume training is the order of the day. The vast majority of exercises are of the multi-joint power type, such as power cleans, power snatches, and other variations of the Olympic lifts, such as hang cleans and high pulls. The number of exercise sets per training session is three throughout the entire phase, indicating, of course, a relatively low volume of training. Intensity is relatively high with, at most, three repetitions per set throughout the peaking phase. Intensity reaches its maximum during weeks three, four and six, when there are only one or two repetitions per set of multi-joint power exercises.

The pattern of heavy, moderate and light training days is varied throughout the phase, with two heavy training days per week in weeks four and five. During week six, there's only one heavy day and one moderate day to allow some recovery after weeks four and five (in which there are two heavy training days per week).

Rest between sets and exercises is relatively long throughout the phase. From week three through week six, four to five-minute rest periods between sets and exercises are allowed. This is to ensure that the trainee can handle the maximal and near-maximal resistances required to peak maximal strength and power prior to the competitive season.

The competition training phase was outlined in Figure 8.8; the weekly variation in training further developed in Figure 9.7. This phase lasts eight weeks. To maintain the maximal strength and power developed in previous training phases, high-intensity/low-volume training is the ticket. Except for weeks six and eight, two training sessions per week are performed. During week six (occurring two weeks prior to the major competition of the season), three training sessions are scheduled. This is followed by two weeks of lower volume training, all the better to help in achieving a peak in strength and power at the exact time of the major competition.

All training in this phase is high intensity with, at most, three repetitions per set for all multi-joint power or multi-joint strength exercises. Intensity is gradually increased throughout the phase with all exercises at the 1 RM level during week eight.

Rest periods are relatively long throughout the phase. Three to four-minute rest periods are allowed in weeks one to four, and four to five-minute periods during weeks five through eight. This is necessary in order to ensure physical and psychological recovery from using at or near 1 RM resistances.

A secondary goal of the relatively small volume of resistance training during the competition season is simply to decrease the amount of training time spent in the weight room. This is done so more training time can be dedicated to the skill training necessary to perfect technique in strength power events.

Figure 9.2

STRENGTH/POWER RECOVERY PHASE

Sport/Activity Strength/Power   **Dates of Training Phase** June 1   **to** June 30

Training Phase Recovery

	Volume/Intensity	Sessions per Week	Number and Type of Exercises	Set/Rep Scheme	Rest Between Sets and Exercises
Week 1	Moderate/Low	2 L	2 MJ, 3 arm, 3 leg, 1 ab	2/10-12	3 min
		L	2 MJ, 3 arm, 3 leg, 1 ab	2/10-12	3 min
					3 min
Week 2	Moderate/Low	2 M	2 MJ, 3 arm, 3 leg, 1 ab	3/10-12	3 min
		L	2 MJ, 3 arm, 3 leg, 1 ab	3/10-12	3 min
Week 3	Moderate/Low	3H	3 MJ, 3 arm, 2 leg, 1 ab, 1 low back	3/10-12	2 min
		M	3 MJ, 3 arm, 2 leg, 1 ab, 1 low back	3/10-12	2 min
		L	3 MJ, 3 arm, 2 leg, 1 ab, 1 low back	3/10-12	2 min
Week 4	Moderate/Low	3H	3 MJ, 3 arm, 2 leg, 1 ab, 1 low back	3/10-12	2 min
		M	3 MJ, 3 arm, 2 leg, 1 ab, 1 low back	3/10-12	2 min
		L	3 MJ, 3 arm, 2 leg, 1 ab, 1 low back	3/10-12	3 min

MJ= Multi-Joint Exercise

Figure 9.2. Strength/power recovery phase.

Figure 9.3

STRENGTH/POWER HYPERTROPHY PHASE

Sport/Activity <u>Strength/Power</u>   **Dates of Training Phase** <u>July 1</u>   **to** <u>August 31</u>

Training Phase <u>Hypertrophy</u>

	Volume/Intensity	Sessions per Week	Number and Type of Exercises	Set/Rep Scheme	Rest Between Sets and Exercises
Week 1	High/Low	3H	3 MJ, 3 arm, 2 leg, 2 ab, 1 low back	3/10 MJ, 3/15 SJ	3 min
		M	3 MJ, 3 arm, 2 leg, 2 ab, 1 low back	3/10 MJ, 3/15 SJ	3 min
		L	3 MJ, 3 arm, 2 leg, 2 ab, 1 low back	3/10 MJ, 3/15 SJ	3 min
Week 2	High/Low	3H	3 MJ, 3 arm, 2 leg, 1 ab, 2 low back	4/10 MJ, 3/15 SJ	2.5 min
		M	3 MJ, 3 arm, 2 leg, 1 ab, 2 low back	4/10 MJ, 3/15 SJ	2.5 min
		L	3 MJ, 3 arm, 2 leg, 1 ab, 2 low back	4/10 MJ, 3/15 SJ	2.5 min
Week 3	High/Low	3H	3 MJ, 3 arm, 2 leg, 2 ab, 2 low back	4/10 MJ, 4/15 SJ	2 min
		M	3 MJ, 3 arm, 2 leg, 2 ab, 2 low back	4/10 MJ, 4/15 SJ	2 min
		L	3 MJ, 3 arm, 2 leg, 2 ab, 2 low back	4/10 MJ, 4/15 SJ	2 min
Week 4	High/Moderate	4H	2 MJ, 1 MJP, 2 arm, 2 leg, 2 ab, 2 low back	4/10 MJ, 4/15 SJ	2 min
		M	2 MJ, 1 MJP, 2 arm, 2 leg, 2 ab, 2 low back	4/10 MJ, 4/15 SJ	2 min
		L	2 MJ, 1 MJP, 2 arm, 2 leg, 2 ab, 2 low back	4/10 MJ, 4/15 SJ	2 min
		M	2 MJ, 1 MJP, 2 arm, 2 leg, 2 ab, 2 low back	4/10 MJ, 4/15 SJ	2 min
Week 5	Moderate/Moderate	4H	3 MJ, 1 MJP, 2 arm, 1 leg, 2 ab, 2 low back	5/8 MJ, 4/12 SJ	2 min
		M	3 MJ, 1 MJP, 2 arm, 1 leg, 2 ab, 2 low back	5/8 MJ, 4/12 SJ	2 min
		L	3 MJ, 1 MJP, 2 arm, 1 leg, 2 ab, 2 low back	5/8 MJ, 4/12 SJ	2 min
		M	3 MJ, 1 MJP, 2 arm, 1 leg, 2 ab, 2 low back	5/8 MJ, 4/12 SJ	2 min
Week 6	Moderate/Moderate	4H	3 MJ, 1 MJP, 2 arm, 2 leg, 2 ab, 2 low back	5/8 MJ, 4/12 SJ	3 min MJ, 1.5 min SJ
		M	3 MJ, 1 MJP, 2 arm, 2 leg, 2 ab, 2 low back	5/8 MJ, 4/12 SJ	3 min MJ, 1.5 min SJ
		L	3 MJ, 1 MJP, 2 arm, 2 leg, 2 ab, 2 low back	5/8 MJ, 4/12 SJ	3 min MJ, 1.5 min SJ
		H	3 MJ, 1 MJP, 2 arm, 2 leg, 2 ab, 2 low back	5/8 MJ, 4/12 SJ	3 min MJ, 1.5 min SJ
Week 7	Moderate/Moderate	4H	3 MJ, 1 MJP, 2 arm, 2 leg, 2 ab, 2 low back	5/8 MJ, 3/12 SJ	3 min MJ, 1.5 min SJ
		M	3 MJ, 1 MJP, 2 arm, 2 leg, 2 ab, 2 low back	5/8 MJ, 3/12 SJ	3 min MJ, 1.5 min SJ
		L	3 MJ, 1 MJP, 2 arm, 2 leg, 2 ab, 2 low back	5/8 MJ, 3/12 SJ	3 min MJ, 1.5 min SJ
		H	3 MJ, 1 MJP, 2 arm, 2 leg, 2 ab, 2 low back	5/8 MJ, 3/12 SJ	3 min MJ, 1.5 min SJ
Week 8	Moderate/High	4H	3 MJ, 1 MJP, 2 arm, 2 leg, 2 ab, 2 low back	4/8 MJ, 3/10 SJ	2 min
		M	3 MJ, 1 MJP, 2 arm, 2 leg, 2 ab, 2 low back	4/8 MJ, 3/10 SJ	2 min
		L	3 MJ, 1 MJP, 2 arm, 2 leg, 2 ab, 2 low back	4/8 MJ, 3/10 SJ	2 min

MJ= Multi-Joint Exercise, SJ=Single-Joint Exercise, MJP= Multi-Joint Power Exercise

Figure 9.3. *Strength/power hypertrophy phase.*

Figure 9.4

STRENGTH/POWER STRENGTH PHASE

Sport/Activity <u>Strength/Power</u>　　　　　　**Dates of Training Phase** <u>September 1</u> **to** <u>September 30</u>

Training Phase <u>Strength</u>

	Volume/Intensity	Sessions per Week	Number and Type of Exercises	Set/Rep Scheme	Rest Between Sets and Exercises
Week 1	High/Moderate-High	4H	4 MJ, 2 MJP, 2 ab, 2 low back	3/6 MJ, 4/8-10 SJ	3 min MJ, 3 min SJ
		M	4 MJ, 2 MJP, 2 ab, 2 low back	3/6 MJ, 4/8-10 SJ	3 min MJ, 3 min SJ
		L	4 MJ, 2 MJP, 2 ab, 2 low back	3/6 MJ, 4/8-10 SJ	3 min MJ, 3 min SJ
		M	4 MJ, 2 MJP, 2 ab, 2 low back	3/6 MJ, 4/8-10 SJ	3 min MJ, 3 min SJ
Week 2	High/High	4H	4 MJ, 2 MJP, 2 ab, 2 low back	5/3-6 MJ, 3/8 SJ	3 min MJ, 2 min SJ
		L	4 MJ, 2 MJP, 2 ab, 2 low back	5/3-6 MJ, 3/8 SJ	3 min MJ, 2 min SJ
		H	4 MJ, 2 MJP, 2 ab, 2 low back	5/3-6 MJ, 3/8 SJ	3 min MJ, 2 min SJ
		M	4 MJ, 2 MJP, 2 ab, 2 low back	5/3-6 MJ, 3/8 SJ	3 min MJ, 2 min SJ
Week 3	Moderate-High/High	3H	4 MJ, 2 MJP, 1 ab, 1 low back	5/2-5 MJ, 3/8 SJ	4 min MJ, 3 min SJ
		M	4 MJ, 2 MJP, 1 ab, 1 low back	5/2-5 MJ, 3/8 SJ	4 min MJ, 3 min SJ
		M	4 MJ, 2 MJP, 1 ab, 1 low back	5/2-5 MJ, 3/8 SJ	4 min MJ, 3 min SJ
Week 4	Moderate/High	3H	4 MJ, 2 MJP, 1 ab, 1 low back	4/2-3 MJ, 3/8 SJ	4 min MJ, 3 min SJ
		L	4 MJ, 2 MJP, 1 ab, 1 low back	4/2-3 MJ, 3/8 SJ	4 min MJ, 3 min SJ
		M	4 MJ, 2 MJP, 1 ab, 1 low back	4/2-3 MJ, 3/8 SJ	4 min MJ, 3 min SJ

MJ= Multi-Joint Exercise, SJ=Single-Joint Exercise, MJP= Multi-Joint Power Exercise

Figure 9.4. Strength/power strength phase.

Figure 9.5

STRENGTH/POWER POWER PHASE

Sport/Activity <u>Strength/Power</u>   **Dates of Training Phase** <u>October 1</u>   **to** <u>October 31</u>

Training Phase <u>Power</u>

	Volume/Intensity	Sessions per Week	Number and Type of Exercises	Set/Rep Scheme	Rest Between Sets and Exercises
Week 1	Moderate-Low/Moderate-High	3H	3 MJP, 2 MJ, 1 ab, 1 low back	5/3 MJ	3-4 min
		L	3 MJP, 2 MJ, 1 ab, 1 low back	5/3 MJ	3-4 min
		M	3 MJP, 2 MJ, 1 ab, 1 low back	5/3 MJ	3-4 min
Week 2	High/High	3H	3 MJP, 2 MJ, 1 ab, 1 low back	5/3 MJ	3-4 min
		M	3 MJP, 2 MJ, 1 ab, 1 low back	5/3 MJ	3-4 min
		M	3 MJP, 2 MJ, 1 ab, 1 low back	5/3 MJ	3-4 min
Week 3	Moderate-High/High	3H	3 MJP, 1 MJ, 1 ab	4-5/2-3 MJ	4 min
		L	3 MJP, 1 MJ, 1 ab	4-5/2-3 MJ	4 min
		H	3 MJP, 1 MJ, 1 ab	4-5/2-3 MJ	4 min
Week 4	Moderate/High	3H	3 MJP, 1 MJ, 1 ab	4-5/2-3 MJ	4 min
		L	3 MJP, 1 MJ, 1 ab	4-5/2-3 MJ	4 min
		H	3 MJP, 1 MJ, 1 ab	4-5/2-3 MJ	4 min

MJ= Multi-Joint Exercise, SJ=Single-Joint Exercise, MJP= Multi-Joint Power Exercise

Figure 9.5. Strength/power power phase.

Figure 9.6

STRENGTH/POWER PEAKING PHASE

Sport/Activity <u>Strength/Power</u> **Dates of Training Phase** <u>February 1</u> **to** <u>April 13</u>

Training Phase <u>Peaking</u>

	Volume/Intensity	Sessions per Week	Number and Type of Exercises	Set/Rep Scheme	Rest Between Sets and Exercises
Week 1	Moderate-Low/High	3H	3 MJP, 2 MJ, 1 ab	3/3 all	3-4 min
		L	3 MJP, 2 MJ, 1 ab	3/3 all	3-4 min
		M	3 MJP, 2 MJ, 1 ab	3/3 all	3-4 min
Week 2	Low/High	3H	3 MJP, 1 MJ, 1 ab	3/2-3 all	3-4 min
		M	3 MJP, 1 MJ, 1 ab	3/2-3 all	3-4 min
		M	3 MJP, 1 MJ, 1 ab	3/2-3 all	3-4 min
Week 3	Low/High	3H	3 MJP, 1 MJ, 1 ab	3/1-2 MJP	4-5 min
		L	3 MJP, 1 MJ, 1 ab	3/1-2 MJP	4-5 min
		M	3 MJP, 1 MJ, 1 ab	3/1-2 MJP	4-5 min
Week 4	Very Low/High	3H	3 MJP, 1 MJ, 1 ab	3/1-2 MJP	4-5 min
		L	3 MJP, 1 MJ, 1 ab	3/1-2 MJP	4-5 min
		H	3 MJP, 1 MJ, 1 ab	3/1-2 MJP	4-5 min
Week 5	Very Low/Very High	2H	3 MJP, 1 MJ, 1 ab	3/2-3 MJP, 3/3 MJ	4-5 min
		H	3 MJP, 1 MJ, 1 ab	3/2-3 MJP, 3/3 MJ	4-5 min
Week 6	Very Low/Very High	2H	2 MJP, 1 MJ, 1 ab	3/1-2 MJP, 3/2 MJ	4-5 min
		M	2 MJP, 1 MJ, 1 ab	3/1-2 MJP, 3/2 MJ	4-5 min

MJ= Multi-Joint Exercise, SJ=Single-Joint Exercise, MJP= Multi-Joint Power Exercise

Figure 9.6. Strength/power peaking phase.

Figure 9.7

STRENGTH/POWER COMPETITIVE PHASE

Sport/Activity Strength/Power   **Dates of Training Phase** April 14 **to** May 29

Training Phase Competition

	Volume/Intensity	Sessions per Week	Number and Type of Exercises	Set/Rep Scheme	Rest Between Sets and Exercises
Week 1	Low/High	2H	3 MJP, 1 MJ, 1 ab	3/3 all	3-4 min
		M	3 MJP, 1 MJ, 1 ab	3/3 all	3-4 min
Week 2	Low/High	3H	3 MJP, 1 MJ, 1 ab	3/2-3 all	3 min
		M	3 MJP, 1 MJ, 1 ab	3/2-3 all	3 min
Week 3	Low/High	2H	2 MJP, 1 MJ, 1 ab	3/2-3 all	3-4 min
		M	2 MJP, 1 MJ, 1 ab	3/2-3 all	3-4 min
Week 4	Low/High	2H	2 MJP, 1 MJ, 1 ab	3/1-3 MJP, 3/3 MJ	3-4 min
		M	3 MJP, 1 MJ, 1 ab	3/1-3 MJP, 3/3 MJ	3-4 min
Week 5	Low/High	2H	2 MJP, 1 MJ, 1 ab	3/1-3 MJP, 3/3 MJ	4-5 min
		M	2 MJP, 1 MJ, 1 ab	3/1-3 MJP, 3/3 MJ	4-5 min
Week 6	Low/High	3H	3 MJP, 1 MJ, 1 ab	3/1-2 MJP, 3/2 MJ	4-5 min
		M	3 MJP, 1 MJ, 1 ab	3/1-2 MJP, 3/2 MJ	4-5 min
		M	3 MJP, 1 MJ, 1 ab	3/1-2 MJP, 3/2 MJ	4-5 min
Week 7	Low/High	2H	2 MJP, 1 MJ, 1 ab	3/1-2, MJP, 3/2 MJ	4-5 min
		M	2 MJP, 1 MJ, 1 ab	3/1-2, MJP, 3/2 MJ	4-5 min
Week 8	Low/High	1H	2 MJP, 1 MJ, 1 ab	3/1 all	4-5 min

MJ= Multi-Joint Exercise, SJ=Single-Joint Exercise, MJP= Multi-Joint Power Exercise

Figure 9.7. Strength/power competition phase.

BASKETBALL TRAINING PLAN

The yearly plan for basketball was developed in Figure 8.9, with each training phase further developed in Figures 8.10 through 8.14.

The basketball hypertrophy phase is eight weeks in length. The weekly variation is further developed in Figure 9.8. In order to induce an increase in muscle size, a large volume of training must be performed. Throughout this phase, relatively high numbers of reps per set are the rule for all exercises.

The majority of weeks follow a heavy, moderate, and light training scheme. However, during weeks six and seven, a heavy, light, heavy training scheme is the order of the day. Due to the utilization of four sets per exercise and two heavy days of training per week, this is clearly the most stressful training period. Volume is decreased during week eight by lowering the number of sets per exercise back down to three (as was the case in weeks one to four). Week eight follows a heavy, moderate, and light training pattern. It should allow some recovery prior to the initiation of the strength phase that follows.

During weeks three through six, the number of repetitions per exercise for single-joint exercises is twelve. This is done to increase total training volume, which should act as a stimulus for increased muscle size. The length of rest periods during week one is three minutes. This is gradually decreased to two minutes, and then to one minute during the last four weeks of training. The shorter rest periods should result in a greater stimulus for an increase in muscle size. During weeks five through eight, a combination of one and two-minute rest periods between sets and exercises is used.

The two-minute rest periods are employed on all heavy and on some moderate training days and, on some training days between sets and exercises that are multi-joint in nature. This is done to allow the use of slightly greater resistances. The one-minute rest periods are for lighter training days and for exercises that are single-joint in nature.

The strength phase of basketball training was outlined in Figure 8.11 and the weekly variation further developed in Figure 9.9. A six-week phase similar to the hypertrophy phase, it employs a heavy, moderate, and light training day scheme most weeks. Weeks three and four, a heavy/moderate/moderate scheme is used to increase training stimulus. The number of multi-joint exercises is gradually increased from four during week one to five during week six. Starting with week three, one to two multi-joint power exercises are thrown in. This is done to increase the power capabilities of the athlete and to prepare him or her for the upcoming power training phase. Abdominal strength is very important for the transfer of leg strength and power to the upper body during total body movements (such as those common to basketball). With this in mind, beginning in week three two abdominal exercises are included in the session instead of one.

Six repetitions per set for multi-joint exercises are scheduled starting in week two, with eight repetitions per set for single-joint exercises. This slightly greater number of repetitions adds variation to the training and acts as a stimulus for continued increases in muscle size.

Rest periods between sets and exercises are three minutes for multi-joint exercises, to allow adequate recovery from resistances used on heavy training days. To decrease the total amount of time spent in the weight room and to act as a stimulus for an increase in muscle size, two-minute rests periods are recommended for single-joint exercises starting in week three and continuing through week six.

The four-week power phase was outlined in Figure 8.12, with further developments in weekly variation depicted in Figure 9.10. The most stressful training occurs during weeks two and three, with two heavy training days per week. The training stimulus used to increase total body strength and power is predominantly multi-joint and multi-joint power exercises. The number of repetitions per set for the multi-joint exercises is relatively low (ranging from six to three), with the number of reps gradually reduced as the phase progresses.

Relatively long rest periods of three or four minutes are the standard throughout for both multi-joint power and multi-joint exercises. Longer rest periods should result in sufficient recovery to allow for heavy resistances. Two-minute rest periods are standard for the few single-joint exercises. This is done both to act as a stimulus to maintain muscle mass and to shorten the total amount of time spent in the weight room.

The recovery phase runs two weeks, as outlined in Figure 8.13, with further development of weekly variation seen in Figure 9.11. Total volume of exercise is quite low. The majority of the exercises are single-joint in nature, with only two sets of each exercise. In week two, two training sessions are engaged in, both light in nature. Rest between sets and exercises: three minutes for multi-joint power exercises and two minutes for all others. Given the small total training volume per session, rest periods of this length will allow enough time to keep stress levels very low and assure that the athlete fully recovers from the previous training phase.

The in-season phase was developed in Figure 8.14 with further weekly variations in Figure 9.12. Due to a perhaps hectic schedule of up to several basketball games per week during the season, the total resistance training volume needs to be kept relatively low. Accordingly, only one or two resistance training sessions are scheduled per week during the season. Multi-joint power and multi-joint strength exercises are used almost exclusively throughout the in-season phase. This is because the goal of the phase is to maintain total body strength and power. Too, multi-joint exercises, as opposed to single-joint exercises, train several muscle groups at one time. This reduces the number of exercises that need to be included in a training session—conserving valuable time—while still providing some training stimulus for all the major muscle groups.

The number of repetitions per set is held constant at six to eight to act as a stimulus to maintain or increase total body strength. Rest periods are two minutes. The major reason for choosing this length is, again, to minimize weight room time. Still, two minutes should allow adequate recovery to use sufficiently heavy resistances and thereby maintain in-season strength. Two to three weeks prior to the start of major tournaments, three training sessions per week can be performed for one to two weeks. This is done to create a conditioning peak during the tournaments.

Figure 9.8

BASKETBALL HYPERTROPHY PHASE

Sport/Activity Basketball   **Dates of Training Phase** April 1 ___ to May 23 ___

Training Phase Hypertrophy

	Volume/Intensity	Sessions per Week	Number and Type of Exercises	Set/Rep Scheme	Rest Between Sets and Exercises
Week 1	Moderate/Low	3M	3 MJ, 3 arm, 4 leg, 1 ab	3/10 all	3 min
		M	3 MJ, 3 arm, 4 leg, 1 ab	3/10 all	3 min
		M	3 MJ, 3 arm, 4 leg, 1 ab	3/10 all	3 min
Week 2	Moderate/Low	3H	3 MJ, 3 arm, 4 leg, 2 ab	3/10 all	3 min
		L	3 MJ, 3 arm, 4 leg, 2 ab	3/10 all	3 min
		M	3 MJ, 3 arm, 4 leg, 2 ab	3/10 all	3 min
Week 3	Moderate-High/Moderate	3H	3 MJ, 3 arm, 4 leg, 1 ab, 1 low back	3/10 MJ, 4/12 SJ	2 min
		L	3 MJ, 3 arm, 4 leg, 1 ab, 1 low back	3/10 MJ, 4/12 SJ	2 min
		M	3 MJ, 3 arm, 4 leg, 1 ab, 1 low back	3/10 MJ, 4/12 SJ	2 min
Week 4	Moderate-High/Moderate	3H	3 MJ, 3 arm, 4 leg, 1 ab, 1 low back	3/10 MJ, 4/12 SJ	2 min
		L			
		M			
Week 5	High/Moderate	3H	4 MJ, 3 arm, 4 leg, 2 ab, 1 low back	4/10 MJ, 3/12 SJ	H & M 2 min
		L			L1 min
		M			
Week 6	High/Moderate	3H	4 MJ, 3 arm, 4 leg, 2 ab, 1 low back	4/10 MJ, 3/12 SJ	H 2 m for MJ, 1 m SJ
		L			L 1 min all
		H			
Week 7	High/High	3H	4 MJ, 2 arm, 2 leg, 2 ab, 1 low back	4/10 all	H 2 min MJ, 1 min SJ
		L			L 1 min all
		H			
Week 8	Moderate-High/Moderate	3H	4 MJ, 2 arm, 2 leg, 1 ab, 1 low back	3/10 all	H 2 min MJ, 1 min SJ
		L			L & M 1 min
		M			

MJ= Multi-Joint Exercise, SJ=Single-Joint Exercise, MJP= Multi-Joint Power Exercise

Figure 9.8. *Basketball hypertrophy phase.*

Figure 9.9

BASKETBALL STRENGTH PHASE

Sport/Activity <u>Basketball</u>   **Dates of Training Phase** <u>May 24</u> **to** <u>July 4</u>

Training Phase <u>Strength</u>

	Volume/Intensity	Sessions per Week	Number and Type of Exercises	Set/Rep Scheme	Rest Between Sets and Exercises
Week 1	High/Moderate	3H	4 MJ, 2 arm, 2 leg, 1 ab, 1 low back	4/8 all	3 min all
		L	4 MJ, 2 arm, 2 leg, 1 ab, 1 low back	4/8 all	3 min all
		M	4 MJ, 2 arm, 2 leg, 1 ab, 1 low back	4/8 all	3 min all
Week 2	Moderate/Moderate	3H	4 MJ, 2 arm, 2 leg, 1 ab, 1 low back	4/6 MJ, 4/8 SJ	3 min all
		L	4 MJ, 2 arm, 2 leg, 1 ab, 1 low back	4/6 MJ, 4/8 SJ	3 min all
		M	4 MJ, 2 arm, 2 leg, 1 ab, 1 low back	4/6 MJ, 4/8 SJ	3 min all
Week 3	Moderate/Moderate-High	3H	1 MJP, 4 MJ, 2 arm, 2 leg, 2 ab	4/6 MJ, 3/8 SJ	3 min MJ, 2 min SJ
		M	1 MJP, 4 MJ, 2 arm, 2 leg, 2 ab	4/6 MJ, 3/8 SJ	3 min MJ, 2 min SJ
		M	1 MJP, 4 MJ, 2 arm, 2 leg, 2 ab	4/6 MJ, 3/8 SJ	3 min MJ, 2 min SJ
Week 4	Moderate-High	3H	2 MJP, 3 MJ, 2 arm, 2 leg, 2 ab	4/6 MJ, 3/8 SJ	3 min MJ, 2 min SJ
		M	2 MJP, 3 MJ, 2 arm, 2 leg, 2 ab	4/6 MJ, 3/8 SJ	3 min MJ, 2 min SJ
		M	2 MJP, 3 MJ, 2 arm, 2 leg, 2 ab	4/6 MJ, 3/8 SJ	3 min MJ, 2 min SJ
Week 5	Moderate-High	3H	2 MJP, 3 MJ, 2 arm, 2 leg, 2 ab	3/6 MJ, 3/8 SJ	3 min MJ, 2 min SJ
		L	2 MJP, 3 MJ, 2 arm, 2 leg, 2 ab	3/6 MJ, 3/8 SJ	3 min MJ, 2 min SJ
		M	2 MJP, 3 MJ, 2 arm, 2 leg, 2 ab	3/6 MJ, 3/8 SJ	3 min MJ, 2 min SJ
Week 6	Moderate-High/Moderate	3H	2 MJP, 3 MJ, 2 arm, 2 leg, 2 ab	3/6 MJ, 3/8 SJ	3 min MJ, 2 min SJ
		L	2 MJP, 3 MJ, 2 arm, 2 leg, 2 ab	3/6 MJ, 3/8 SJ	3 min MJ, 2 min SJ
		M	2 MJP, 3 MJ, 2 arm, 2 leg, 2 ab	3/6 MJ, 3/8 SJ	3 min MJ, 2 min SJ

MJ= Multi-Joint Exercise, SJ=Single-Joint Exercise, MJP= Multi-Joint Power Exercise

Figure 9.9. *Basketball strength phase.*

Figure 9.10

BASKETBALL POWER PHASE

Sport/Activity <u>Basketball</u>   **Dates of Training Phase** <u>July 5</u>   **to** <u>August 1</u>

Training Phase <u>Power</u>

	Volume/Intensity	Sessions per Week	Number and Type of Exercises	Set/Rep Scheme	Rest Between Sets and Exercises
Week 1	High/ Low	3H	2 MJP, 3 MJ, 2 arm, 2 ab	4/5 MJP, 4/6 MJ, 3/6 SJ	3 min MJP & MJ, 2 min SJ
		L	2 MJP, 3 MJ, 2 arm, 2 ab	4/5 MJP, 4/6 MJ, 3/6 SJ	3 min MJP & MJ, 2 min SJ
		M	2 MJP, 3 MJ, 2 arm, 2 ab	4/5 MJP, 4/6 MJ, 3/6 SJ	3 min MJP & MJ, 2 min SJ
Week 2	Moderate/High	3H	3 MJP, 2 MJ, 2 ab, 1 arm	4/3-4 MJP, 4/5 MJ, 3/6 SJ	3 min MJP & MJ, 2 min SJ
		L	3 MJP, 2 MJ, 2 ab, 1 arm	4/3-4 MJP, 4/5 MJ, 3/6 SJ	3 min MJP & MJ, 2 min SJ
		H	3 MJP, 2 MJ, 2 ab, 1 arm	4/3-4 MJP, 4/5 MJ, 3/6 SJ	3 min MJP & MJ, 2 min SJ
Week 3	Moderate /High	3H	3 MJP, 2 MJ, 1 ab, 1 arm	4/3 MJP, 3/3-4 MJ, 2/6 SJ	4 min MJP & MJ, 2 min SJ
		L	3 MJP, 2 MJ, 1 ab, 1 arm	4/3 MJP, 3/3-4 MJ, 2/6 SJ	4 min MJP & MJ, 2 min SJ
		H	3 MJP, 2 MJ, 1 ab, 1 arm	4/3 MJP, 3/3-4 MJ, 2/6 SJ	4 min MJP & MJ, 2 min SJ
Week 4	Low/Moderate	3H	3 MJP, 2 MJ, 1 ab	4/3 MJP, 3/3 MJ, 2/6 SJ	4 min all
		L	3 MJP, 2 MJ, 1 ab	4/3 MJP, 3/3 MJ, 2/6 SJ	4 min all
		M	3 MJP, 2 MJ, 1 ab	4/3 MJP, 3/3 MJ, 2/6 SJ	4 min all

MJ= Multi-Joint Exercise, SJ=Single-Joint Exercise, MJP= Multi-Joint Power Exercise

Figure 9.10. Basketball power phase.

Figure 9.11

BASKETBALL RECOVERY PHASE

Sport/Activity Basketball   **Dates of Training Phase** August 2   to August 15

Training Phase Recovery

	Volume/Intensity	Sessions per Week	Number and Type of Exercises	Set/Rep Scheme	Rest Between Sets and Exercises
Week 1	High-High	3H	1 MJP, 2 MJ, 2 arm, 2 leg, 2 ab, 1 low back	3/6 MJP, 3/10 MJ, 2/12 SJ	3 min MJP,
					2 min all other
		L	1 MJP, 2 MJ, 2 arm, 2 leg, 2 ab, 1 low back	3/6 MJP, 3/10 MJ, 2/12 SJ	3 min MJP,
					2 min all other
		M	1 MJP, 2 MJ, 2 arm, 2 leg, 2 ab, 1 low back	3/6 MJP, 3/10 MJ, 2/12 SJ	3 min MJ, 3 min SJ
Week 2	Low/Low	2L	1 MJP, 3 MJ, 1 arm, 2 leg, 1 ab, 1 low back	3/6 MJP, 2/10 MJ & SJ	3 min MJP,
					2 min all other
		L	1 MJP,3 MJ,1 arm, 2 leg, 1 ab,1 low back	3/6 MJP, 2/10 MJ & SJ	3 min MJP,
					2 min all other

MJ= Multi-Joint Exercise, SJ=Single-Joint Exercise, MJP= Multi-Joint Power Exercise

Figure 9.11. Basketball recovery phase.

Figure 9.12

BASKETBALL IN-SEASON PHASE

Sport/Activity Basketball   **Dates of Training Phase** December 15 to March 30

Training Phase In-Season

	Volume/Intensity	Sessions per Week	Number and Type of Exercises	Set/Rep Scheme	Rest Between Sets and Exercises
Week 1	All Moderate/Moderate	1-2 Normally	1 MJP, 4-5 MJ, 1 ab, 1 low back	3/6 MJP	2 min all
		M		3/8-10 MJ	
		M			
Week 2	2-3 Weeks Prior to	3H	2 MJP, 4 MJ	3/6 MJP	3 min MJP, 2 min MJ
	Start of Tournaments	L	1 ab	3/8 MJ	
		M			

MJ= Multi-Joint Exercise, MJP= Multi-Joint Power Exercise

Figure 9.12. Basketball in-season phase.

See Figures 8.15 through 8.19 for the earlier evolution of this plan. The hypertrophy I training phase was outlined in Figure 8.16, the weekly training variation is further developed in Figure 9.13.

Four weeks in length—as are all the phases that make up the general fitness periodization plan—there are three training sessions per week throughout. Weeks one and two consist of two moderate days of training and one light day. This helps in allowing the lifter to become accustomed to the training. Thereafter, the weekly training variation follows a heavy, moderate and light training day scheme.

Training becomes more stressful as the phase progresses. Several training variables are manipulated in order to make this possible. The total number of exercises per training session is gradually increased from week one through week four. The number of sets for each exercise is gradually increased from one during week one to three during week four. The number of reps per set is relatively high over the course of the phase. The first two weeks, the number of repetitions per set is 20; during weeks three and four it's fifteen. Rest periods are gradually decreased from three minutes during week one to one minute during week four. The use of light resistances allows for the reduction in rest without dramatic effect on resistances used. These manipulations make training more stressful as the phase progresses, and should prepare the trainee for future phases, and act as a stimulus to increase muscle mass.

The hypertrophy II phase was generally developed in Figure 8.17; the weekly training variation is further evolved in Figure 9.14. The hypertrophy II phase is more stressful than the hypertrophy I phase. This design results in greater stimulus for an increase in muscle size.

Notably different than the hypertrophy I phase, II does not have that initial two-week training period during which the lifter can become accustomed to the training stimulus. There are three training sessions per week throughout phase II, with a heavy, moderate, and light weekly pattern. Two minutes of rest are allowed between sets and exercises during week one. The rest between single-joint sets and exercises decreases to one minute by week two, and is maintained at one minute for the remainder of the training phase. Two minutes rest between sets and exercises are allowed for all multi-joint exercises at all times.

The number of repetitions per set for single-joint exercises is 15, as it was during the last two weeks of the hypertrophy I phase. But this time the number of repetitions per multi-joint exercises is decreased to 12 during week two, and maintained at this level. This relatively high-volume training with relatively short rest periods should result in an increase of muscle size, which is the idea. In fact, the training stimulus as outlined should also result in a significant increase in strength as the phase progresses.

Next comes the hypertrophy-strength training phase (see Figure 8.18) and the weekly training variation (see Figure 9.15). The major difference between this phase and the hypertrophy II phase is the decrease in the number of repetitions per set. This allows the trainee to use heavier resistances than during the hypertrophy II phase, resulting in greater stimulus for an increase in—you guessed it—strength and muscle size.

Rest periods are maintained at two minutes between sets and exercises for multi-joint exercises and one minute between sets and exercises for single-joint ones. The longer rest periods for exercises that are multi-joint allows the trainee more recovery time, and permits the utilization of heavier resistances.

Weeks two and three reflect the highest volume of training. Volume is then reduced slightly during week four to allow some recovery prior to the upcoming strength training phase.

The strength training phase was developed in Figure 8.19, and the weekly variation thereof further developed in Figure 9.16. The major difference between this phase and the hypertrophy/strength phase is the smaller total training volume. This is accomplished by the utilization of predominately multi-joint exercises, a decrease in the number of repetitions per set, and an increase in the length of rest periods between sets and exercises. During weeks three and four, multi-joint exercises are performed almost exclusively. Six repetitions per set are utilized with four-minute rest periods interspersed between sets and exercises. The name of the game here is maximal development of total body strength.

Figure 9.13

GENERAL FITNESS HYPERTROPHY I

Sport/Activity General Fitness   **Dates of Training Phase** January 1 **to** January 31

Training Phase Hypertrophy I

	Volume/Intensity	Sessions per Week	Number and Type of Exercises	Set/Rep Scheme	Rest Between Sets and Exercises
Week 1	High/ Low	3M	3 MJ, 2 arm, 2 leg, 1 ab	1/20 all	3 min
		L	3 MJ, 2 arm, 2 leg, 1 ab	1/20 all	3 min
		M	3 MJ, 2 arm, 2 leg, 1 ab	1/20 all	3 min
Week 2	High/ Low	3M	3 MJ, 3 arm, 2 leg, 1 ab	2/20 all	2 min
		L	3 MJ, 3 arm, 2 leg, 1 ab	2/20 all	2 min
		M	3 MJ, 3 arm, 2 leg, 1 ab	2/20 all	2 min
Week 3	High/ Low	3H	3 MJ, 3 arm, 2 leg, 1 ab, 1 low back	2/15 all	2 min MJ, 1 min all other
		L	3 MJ, 3 arm, 2 leg, 1 ab, 1 low back	2/15 all	2 min MJ, 1 min all other
		M	3 MJ, 3 arm, 2 leg, 1 ab, 1 low back	2/15 all	2 min MJ, 1 min all other
Week 4	High/ Low	3H	3 MJ, 4 arm, 3 leg, 1 ab, 1 low back	3/15 all	1 min all
		L	3 MJ, 4 arm, 3 leg, 1 ab, 1 low back	3/15 all	1 min all
		M	3 MJ, 4 arm, 3 leg, 1 ab, 1 low back	3/15 all	1 min all

MJ= Multi-Joint Exercise

Figure 9.13. General fitness hypertrophy I.

Figure 9.14

GENERAL FITNESS HYPERTROPHY II

Sport/Activity General Fitness   **Dates of Training Phase** February 1 **to** February 28

Training Phase Hypertrophy II

	Volume/Intensity	Sessions per Week	Number and Type of Exercises	Set/Rep Scheme	Rest Between Sets and Exercises
Week 1	Moderate-High/Moderate-Low	3H	4 MJ, 3 arm, 4 leg, 1 ab	4/15 all	2 min
		L	4 MJ, 3 arm, 4 leg, 1 ab	4/15 all	2 min
		M	4 MJ, 3 arm, 4 leg, 1 ab	4/15 all	2 min
Week 2	Moderate-High/Moderate-Low	3H	4 MJ, 3 arm, 4 leg, 1 ab, 1 low back	4/12 MJ, 4/15 SJ	2 min MJ, 1 min SJ
		L	4 MJ, 3 arm, 4 leg, 1 ab, 1 low back	4/12 MJ, 4/15 SJ	2 min MJ, 1 min SJ
		M	4 MJ, 3 arm, 4 leg, 1 ab, 1 low back	4/12 MJ, 4/15 SJ	2 min MJ, 1 min SJ
Week 3	Moderate-High/Moderate-Low	3H	4 MJ, 3 arm, 4 leg, 1 ab, 1 low back	4/12 MJ, 5/15 SJ	2 min MJ, 1 min SJ
		L	4 MJ, 3 arm, 4 leg, 1 ab, 1 low back	4/12 MJ, 5/15 SJ	2 min MJ, 1 min SJ
		M	4 MJ, 3 arm, 4 leg, 1 ab, 1 low back	4/12 MJ, 5/15 SJ	2 min MJ, 1 min SJ
Week 4	Moderate-High/Moderate-Low	3H	4 MJ, 3 arm, 4 leg, 1 ab, 1 low back	4/12 MJ, 5/15 SJ	2 min MJ, 1 min SJ
		L	4 MJ, 3 arm, 4 leg, 1 ab, 1 low back	4/12 MJ, 5/15 SJ	2 min MJ, 1 min SJ
		M	4 MJ, 3 arm, 4 leg, 1 ab, 1 low back	4/12 MJ, 5/15 SJ	2 min MJ, 1 min SJ

MJ= Multi-Joint Exercise, SJ=Single-Joint Exercise

Figure 9.14. General fitness hypertrophy II.

Figure 9.15

GENERAL FITNESS HYPERTROPHY/STRENGTH PHASE

Sport/Activity <u>General Fitness</u>   **Dates of Training Phase** <u>March 1</u>   **to** <u>March 31</u>

Training Phase <u>Hypertrophy/Strength</u>

	Volume/Intensity	Sessions per Week	Number and Type of Exercises	Set/Rep Scheme	Rest Between Sets and Exercises
Week 1	Moderate/Moderate	3H	4 MJ, 2 arm, 2 leg, 1 ab	4/10 MJ, 4/12 SJ	2 min MJ, 1 min SJ
		L	4 MJ, 2 arm, 2 leg, 1 ab	4/10 MJ, 4/12 SJ	2 min MJ, 1 min SJ
		M	4 MJ, 2 arm, 2 leg, 1 ab	4/10 MJ, 4/12 SJ	2 min MJ, 1 min SJ
Week 2	Moderate/Moderate	3H	4 MJ, 2 arm, 2 leg, 1 ab	5/10 MJ, 4/12 SJ	2 min MJ, 1 min SJ
		L	4 MJ, 2 arm, 2 leg, 1 ab	5/10 MJ, 4/12 SJ	2 min MJ, 1 min SJ
		M	4 MJ, 2 arm, 2 leg, 1 ab	5/10 MJ, 4/12 SJ	2 min MJ, 1 min SJ
Week 3	Moderate/Moderate	3H	4 MJ, 2 arm, 1 leg, 1 ab	5/10 MJ, 4/12 SJ	2 min MJ, 1 min SJ
		L	4 MJ, 2 arm, 1 leg, 1 ab	5/10 MJ, 4/12 SJ	2 min MJ, 1 min SJ
		M	4 MJ, 2 arm, 1 leg, 1 ab	5/10 MJ, 4/12 SJ	2 min MJ, 1 min SJ
Week 4	Moderate/Moderate	3H	4 MJ, 2 arm, 1 leg, 1 ab	4/10 MJ, 3/12 SJ	2 min MJ, 1 min SJ
		L	4 MJ, 2 arm, 1 leg, 1 ab	4/10 MJ, 3/12 SJ	2 min MJ, 1 min SJ
		M	4 MJ, 2 arm, 1 leg, 1 ab	4/10 MJ, 3/12 SJ	2 min MJ, 1 min SJ

MJ= Multi-Joint Exercise, SJ=Single-Joint Exercise

Figure 9.15. General fitness hypertrophy/strength phase.

Figure 9.16

GENERAL FITNESS STRENGTH PHASE

Sport/Activity <u>General Fitness</u>   **Dates of Training Phase** <u>April 1</u>   **to** <u>April 30</u>

Training Phase <u>Strength</u>

	Volume/Intensity	Sessions per Week	Number and Type of Exercises	Set/Rep Scheme	Rest Between Sets and Exercises
Week 1	Low/High	3H	5 MJ, 1 arm, 1 leg, 1 ab	4/8 MJ, 3/8 SJ	3 min MJ, 2 min SJ
		L	5 MJ, 1 arm, 1 leg, 1 ab	4/8 MJ, 3/8 SJ	3 min MJ, 2 min SJ
		M	5 MJ, 1 arm, 1 leg, 1 ab	4/8 MJ, 3/8 SJ	3 min MJ, 2 min SJ
Week 2	Low/High	3H	5 MJ, 1 arm, 1 leg, 1 ab	5/8 MJ, 3/8 SJ	3 min MJ, 2 min SJ
		L	5 MJ, 1 arm, 1 leg, 1 ab	5/8 MJ, 3/8 SJ	3 min MJ, 2 min SJ
		M	5 MJ, 1 arm, 1 leg, 1 ab	5/8 MJ, 3/8 SJ	3 min MJ, 2 min SJ
Week 3	Low/High	3H	5 MJ, 1 ab	5/6 MJ	4 min
		L	5 MJ, 1 ab	5/6 MJ	4 min
		M	5 MJ, 1 ab	5/6 MJ	4 min
Week 4	Low/High	3H	5 MJ, 1 ab	5/6 MJ	4 min
		L	5 MJ, 1 ab	5/6 MJ	4 min
		M	5 MJ, 1 ab	5/6 MJ	4 min

MJ= Multi-Joint Exercise, SJ=Single-Joint Exercise

Figure 9.16. *General fitness strength phase.*

Naturally, there are many other possible variations within any of the training phases discussed in this chapter. Whatever the variation, the important factor is careful planning. Vital to this process is keeping the goals, training objectives, and needs of the individual in mind. It all comes down to you, and the special needs and developing capabilities of your body. In chapter 10, the weekly training plan will be used to develop individual training sessions.

We're getting there!

designing one training session

after developing the weekly training outline in chapter 9, it may seem there are no further important decisions to be made. No way! Now the exact exercises in each training session must be determined. The order in which said exercises will be performed must also be determined—as well as whether you'll use a machine, barbell, dumbbell, or a combination of training devices.

Perhaps the most difficult decision yet to be made is what weight or resistance you'll use for each set. After considering individual needs and goals, exercise choice and the exercise order is a much easier decision for most people. Choosing the right resistance can be especially difficult because of the limitless number of sets, repetitions, and weight schemes possible.

Should the same weight be used for all sets in a session? Should the weight used be a repetition maximum resistance? The question of how much weight or resistance to use for a particular set of an exercise becomes even more complicated when the training scheme involves heavy, moderate, and light days.

However, a weight or weights obviously must be chosen. As general guideline, on heavy training days use 95-100 percent of the RM for the desired number of repetitions; on moderate training days, use 85-95 percent; and on light training days, 75-85 percent. If, for example, an athlete wants ten-repetition sets, and the maximum weight he can lift ten times for a particular exercise is 100 pounds, his 10 RM is 100 pounds. Therefore, for this exercise on light days, use 75-85 pounds; on moderate days, use 85-95 pounds; and on heavy days use 95-100 pounds. These weights can then be adjusted to meet the strength and fitness level of each lifter, so that relatively heavy, moderate and light days can be scheduled. The percentage may vary from exercise to exercise. Thus, 90 percent of the RM may be used for one exercise and 85 percent used for another exercise in the same session. During some heavy sessions the desired number of reps per set may not be achieved. This is alright, since the effect you're really trying to achieve is called a training zone.

In general, the training zone is *the desired number of repetitions plus or minus two repetitions.* So, if the program calls for 10 repetitions in three sets, the lifter might actually do 10, nine and eight repetitions in the three sets. If the lifter is consistently out of the desired training zone, the weights should be adjusted as soon as possible.

There is no one hard and fast rule concerning how much weight or resistance should be used for a particular number of repetitions. (When is life ever that simple!) Nor is there any universally accepted sport science research data to substantiate exactly how much resistance should be used. All of these decisions must be based on the knowledge and experience of the person designing the training program, using all the information presented in this book. It's called using good training judgment. All the available research information must be carefully weighed and skillfully applied to the individual's situation. Just as your physician treats you with the latest medical advances, there is an art to intelligently interpreting the most up-to-date information and designing an excellent individual program based on objective critical appraisal.

TRAINING SESSION PLANNING AND RECORD FORM

The use of a form similar to Figure 10.1 is important in planning your training session and recording what was actually performed during a session.

"Sport/Activity" and "Training Phase" are designations already familiar to you. "Week" refers, of course, to whatever week in the training phase the session falls. And "Date" refers, as you know, to the actual day on which the training session will be performed. "Exercises" is nothing more than a list of the exercises to be performed, in order. "Planned Sets x Reps at Weight" refers to the planned number of sets, repetitions, and the resistance to be used for each exercise in the session. "Actual Sets x Reps at Weight" refers to what was in fact performed that day.

You'll find that—when it comes to imperfect human beings—planning and execution can often differ, sometimes rather substantially. For example, you may have intended to perform four sets of 10 repetitions at 100 pounds for a particular exercise. However, in reality, four sets of 10, 10, 8, and 7 repetitions were performed using 100 pounds. This is important information when charting future training sessions, and should be duly recorded. The "Rest Between Sets and Exercises" designation is self-explanatory. Here again, intended rest periods and actual rest periods may vary.

Figure 10.1

TRAINING SESSION PLANNING AND RECORD FORM

Sport/Activity _____   Week _____

Training Phase _____   Date _____

Exercises	Planned Sets x Reps at Weight	Actual Sets x Reps at Weight

Rest Between Sets and Exercises: _____

Comments: _____

_____

Figure 10.1. Training session planning and record form.

The "Comments" section consists of any information that may be pertinent to the planning of future sessions. You might note, let's say, that it's time to increase the resistance for the bench press. But any comments you care to make are important when it comes to considering future workout modifications. It could also be noted if you felt pain when performing a particular exercise—and that a substitute exercise should probably be used.

In this chapter, Figure 10.1 will be completed for a given training session in the first and last week of each training phase in the strength/power, basketball and general fitness yearly training plans. It is important to remember that all training sessions in week one—or any week—of a training phase will vary slightly. The goal here is to discuss how to plan a training session and how the sessions will progress from week one to the last week within each training phase.

The exact weight used for each set of an exercise in a training session will vary tremendously from individual to individual. However, an applicable generalization such as "use the same weight for all training sets of an exercise" will be included in our breakdown of each training session. In general, when resistance is discussed, it refers to heavy training days. On light and moderate training days, the resistance, by definition, would be less.

Many of the decisions needed to plan one training session have already been made—and fully discussed—in chapter 9. The appropriate Figure in chapter 9 describing the development of each weekly training phase should be referred to when considering the development of an individual training session.

While planning your training sessions is very important, until the session is actually history, it's never too late to make minor adjustments in the plan, if they are warranted. Periodized training allows you to be flexible. That is, indeed, one of its greatest advantages.

STRENGTH/POWER TRAINING PLAN

The strength/power recovery phase was outlined in Figure 9.2, and a week one training session developed in Figure 10.2. The session begins with two multi-joint exercises. Exercises throughout the session alternate body parts (arm to leg, arm to abdomen) in an attempt to minimize total training stress. Alternate exercise order allows body parts to recover in effective fashion. The total volume of work is relatively low, with only two sets of each exercise. The weight for each set of an exercise remains the same and should allow for successful completion of all repetitions. This is done to ensure that effective recovery occurs not just within this phase, but from the stress of previous phases as well.

A training session from week four of the recovery phase is presented in Figure 10.3. Here, the back squat and standing calf raise are performed, whereas in week one the leg press and donkey calf raise are used. This change was made to relieve stress on the lower back during the initial portion of the recovery phase. Many times with strength/power athletes, the lower back is an area in great need of recovery, due to the performance of heavy-resistance whole body lifts in previous training phases. The number of repetitions for multi-joint exercises is decreased to 10 in week four, so that the intensity is slightly greater compared to week one. The total volume of training is increased by the inclusion of three sets of each exercise in week four as compared to two sets in week one. In addition, the session is made more stressful by decreasing the rest periods between sets and exercises to two minutes in week four as compared to three minutes in week one. Still, the resistance used in week four should allow completion of the desired number of repetitions in all sets.

Figure 10.2

WEEK ONE SESSION OF STRENGTH/POWER RECOVERY PHASE

Sport/Activity <u>Strength/Power</u>　　　　　**Week** <u>1</u>

Training Phase <u>Recovery</u>　　　　　**Date** <u>June 1-7</u>

Exercises	Planned Sets x Reps at Weight	Actual Sets x Reps at Weight
Leg Press (MJ)	2 x 12 at	
Bench Press (MJ)	2 x 12 at	
Knee Curl (leg)	2 x 12 at	
Triceps Extension (arm)	2 x 12 at	
Donkey Calf Raise (leg)	2 x 12 at	
Elbow Curl (arm)	2 x 12 at	
Hip Abduction/Adduction (leg)	2 x 12 at	
Wrist Curl (arm)	2 x 12 at	
Crunch (ab)	2 x 20	

Rest Between Sets and Exercises: <u>3 minutes all exercises.</u>

Comments: <u>Use weights that allow desired number of reps for both sets.</u>

MJ= Multi-Joint Exercise

Figure 10.2. Week one session of strength/power recovery phase.

Figure 10.3

WEEK FOUR SESSION OF STRENGTH/POWER RECOVERY PHASE

Sport/Activity Strength/Power

Training Phase Recovery

Week 4

Date June 24-30

Exercises	Planned Sets x Reps at Weight	Actual Sets x Reps at Weight
Back Squat (MJ)	3 x 10 at	
Bench Press (MJ)	3 x 10 at	
Seated Row (MJ)	3 x 10 at	
Knee Curl (leg)	3 x 12 at	
Triceps Extension (arm)	3 x 12 at	
Standing Calf Raise (leg)	3 x 12 at	
Elbow Curl (arm)	3 x 12 at	
Wrist Curl (arm)	3 x 12 at	
Back Extensions (low back)	3 x 15 at	
Twisting Crunch (ab)	3 x 20	

Rest Between Sets and Exercises: 2 minutes all exercises.

Comments:

MJ= Multi-Joint Exercise

Figure 10.3. Week four session of strength/power recovery phase.

Weekly variation of the strength/power hypertrophy phase was developed in Figure 9.3. A week one session of the strength/power hypertrophy phase is developed further still in Figure 10.4. Multi-joint exercises are performed first. The stiff-leg dead lift is considered to be a lower back exercise. Although the upright row and lat pulldown are multi-joint exercises—and are performed for three sets of 10 repetitions— they are counted as arm exercises in this training session. Three minutes of rest are allowed between sets and exercises, although, if the athlete is feeling good when performing the single-joint exercises, it is possible these rest periods can be shortened. During the first week of this phase, exercises are alternated between body parts to allow more recovery time between training a particular body part. As the phase continues, it would be possible to stack exercises back-to-back for a particular body part, to make the training more stressful.

A week eight training session for the strength/power hypertrophy phase is developed in Figure 10.5. This training session consists of one multi-joint power exercise (the power clean), and three multi-joint exercises. The power clean is first up in the session, for only six repetitions per set as compared to eight for all other multi-joint exercises. This should allow the athlete to concentrate on development of maximal power during the power clean. The multi-joint exercises are then alternated as much as possible between the upper and lower body. This should allow more recovery when compared to performing two lower body exercises or two upper body exercises back-to-back. The resistance used throughout this phase should make performance of the desired number of repetitions difficult on heavy training days. Rest periods are two minutes—relatively short, considering the large number of multi-joint exercises. Therefore, if needed, the rest periods may be lengthened slightly toward the end of the session to allow the trainee sufficient recovery time.

Figure 10.4

WEEK ONE SESSION OF STRENGTH/POWER HYPERTROPHY PHASE

Sport/Activity Strength/Power

Week 1

Training Phase Hypertrophy

Date July 1-7

Exercises	Planned Sets x Reps at Weight	Actual Sets x Reps at Weight
Back Squat (MJ)	3 x 10 at	
Bench Press (MJ)	3 x 10 at	
Stiff Leg Deadlift (low back)	3 x 10 at	
Lat Pulldown (arm)	3 x 10 at	
Standing Knee Curl (leg)	3 x 15 at	
Knee Extension (leg)	3 x 15 at	
Upright Row (arm)	3 x 10 at	
Dumbbell Elbow Curl (arm)	3 x 15 at	
Triceps Extension (arm)	3 x 15 at	
Twisting Crunch (ab)	3 x 20	
Bent Leg Sit-ups Using Sit-up Board (ab)	3 x 20	

Rest Between Sets and Exercises: 3 minutes all exercises, shorter if feeling good.

Comments:

MJ= Multi-Joint Exercise

Figure 10.4. *Week one session of strength/power hypertrophy phase.*

Figure 10.5

WEEK EIGHT SESSION OF STRENGTH/POWER HYPERTROPHY PHASE

Sport/Activity Strength/Power

Week 8

Training Phase Hypertrophy

Date August 25-31

Exercises	Planned Sets x Reps at Weight	Actual Sets x Reps at Weight
Power Clean (MJP)	4 x 6 at	
Back Squat (MJ)	4 x 8 at	
Bench Press (MJ)	4 x 8 at	
Deadlift (MJ)	4 x 8 at	
Lat Pulldown (arm)	3 x 10 at	
Dip (arm)	3 x 10 at	
Knee Curl (leg)	3 x 10 at	
Donkey Calf (leg)	3 x 10 at	
Good Mornings (low back)	3 x 10 at	
Back Extension (low back)	3 x 15 at	
Crunch (ab)	3 x 20 at	
Twisting Crunch (ab)	3 x 20 at	

Rest Between Sets and Exercises: 2 minutes all sets and exercises, lengthen if needed near end of session.

Comments: Use added weight for back extensions and crunches if needed.

MJ= Multi-Joint Exercise, MJP= Multi-Joint Power Exercise

Figure 10.5. Week eight session of strength/power hypertrophy phase.

The four week strength phase was outlined in Figure 9.4. A week one training session of the phase can be seen in Figure 10.6. The session begins with two multi-joint power exercises performed for three sets of six repetitions. These are followed by the more strength-oriented multi-joint exercises, performed for four sets of eight repetitions. The stiff-leg dead lift is considered a lower back exercise in this training session, but is treated like a multi-joint exercise in terms of reps and sets: therefore, it's performed for four sets of eight repetitions. Many strength/power events such as the shot-put and discus require a twisting motion. Accordingly, one of our abdominal exercises is twisting sit-ups. Three minutes rest is taken between all sets and exercises, although rest periods can be decreased slightly towards the end of the workout for abdominal and lower back exercises.

A training session in the fourth week of the strength/power strength phase in outlined in Figure 10.7. The session starts with two power-oriented exercises for two or three repetitions per set. This should allow the athlete to truly concentrate on the development of maximal power. In addition, the snatch pulls are initiated from knee height, rather than having the bar sitting on the floor. This will more closely mimic the true position from which many strength/power athletes initiate the development of power. Also, many strength/power athletes are behooved to develop strength and power independently in each arm. With this is mind, rather than performing a barbell bench press, we employ the bench press with dumbbells, so that each arm acts independently of the other. The practice of using dumbbells instead of a barbell could also be suited to the execution of the incline press during later portions of this phase.

The resistance used for all heavy training days should make completion of the desired number of repetitions difficult. The resistance used on moderate training days should be 90 to 95% of repetition maximum, and on light days 85 to 90% of that used on heavy training days. Four-minute rests are allowed between sets and exercises of multi-joint power exercises and three-minute rests for multi-joint strength-oriented type exercises. The longer rest periods when performing multi-joint power exercises should allow the athlete sufficient time for recovery, so that maximal power can be developed during each rep of each set.

Figure 10.6

WEEK ONE SESSION OF STRENGTH/POWER STRENGTH PHASE

Sport/Activity Strength/Power   **Week** 1

Training Phase Strength   **Date** September 1-7

Exercises	Planned Sets x Reps at Weight	Actual Sets x Reps at Weight
Snatch Pulls (MJP)	3 x 6 at	
Power Clean (MJP)	3 x 6 at	
Back Squat (MJ)	4 x 8 at	
Back Press (MJ)	4 x 8 at	
Bent Over Row (MJ)	4 x 8 at	
Incline Press (MJ)	4 x 8 at	
Stiff Leg Dead Lift (low back)	4 x 8 at	
Twisting Sit-ups on Decline Board (ab)	3 x 20	
Good Mornings (low back)	3 x 15 at	
Crunches (ab)	3 x 20 at	

Rest Between Sets and Exercises: 3 minutes all sets and exercises.

Comments: _____

MJ= Multi-Joint Exercise, MJP= Multi-Joint Power Exercise

Figure 10.6. Week one session of strength/power strength phase.

Figure 10.7

WEEK FOUR SESSION OF STRENGTH/POWER STRENGTH PHASE

Sport/Activity Strength/Power   **Week** 4

Training Phase Strength   **Date** September 24-30

Exercises	Planned Sets x Reps at Weight	Actual Sets x Reps at Weight
Clean Pull (MJP)	4 x 2 at	
Snatch Pulls From Knees (MJP)	4 x 3 at	
Back Squat (MJ)	4 x 3 at	
Dumbbell Bench Press (MJ)	4 x 5 at	
Incline Press (MJ)	4 x 3 at	
Seated Row (MJ)	4 x 5 at	
Good Mornings (low back)	4 x 8 at	
Twisting Incline Sit-up (ab)	3 x 20	

Rest Between Sets and Exercises: 4 minutes for MJP and 3 minutes for MJ.

Comments: _____

MJ= Multi-Joint Exercise, MJP= Multi-Joint Power Exercise

Figure 10.7. Week four session of strength/power strength phase.

Figure 9.5 outlines the weekly variation for the strength/power power phase. A week one training session for this phase is outlined in Figure 10.8. The goal is to develop maximal power. Therefore, all sessions in this phase are composed primarily of power-oriented type exercises. The session in week one begins with three multi-joint power exercises for five sets of three repetitions. These exercises are followed by multi-joint exercises, also for five sets of three. The session ends with abdominal and lower back exercises. The small number of repetitions per set and the relatively long rest periods of four minutes between power-oriented exercises should allow the athlete to develop maximal power during each repetition of each set. Although the training plan calls for five sets of three repetitions for all multi-joint exercises, it was decided to use five repetitions per set for the dumbbell bench press. Dumbbells instead of a barbell are used for the bench press because many power-oriented athletes must develop strength and power independently in each arm. Dumbbells mimic this development process to a greater extent than barbells.

A week four training session for the strength/power power phase in outlined in Figure 10.9. The training session is composed entirely of multi-joint power/multi-joint exercises plus one abdominal exercise. All exercises except the abdominal exercise are performed for two or three repetitions per set. This will allow the trainee to use very heavy resistances for the desired number of repetitions on the heaviest training days, so that maximal strength and power are developed. Due to the stress applied to the lower back and the number of multi-joint exercises, no additional lower back exercises are included in this session. The rest periods of four minutes between sets and exercises should allow sufficient recovery so that heavy resistances can be used for all sets of the multi-joint exercises.

Figure 10.8

WEEK ONE SESSION OF STRENGTH/POWER POWER PHASE

Sport/Activity <u>Strength/Power</u>   **Week** <u>1</u>

Training Phase <u>Power</u>   **Date** <u>October 1-7</u>

Exercises	Planned Sets x Reps at Weight	Actual Sets x Reps at Weight
Power Clean (MJP)	5 x 3 at	
Snatch Pull (MJP)	5 x 3 at	
Push Jerk (MJP)	5 x 3 at	
Squat (MJ)	5 x 3 at	
Dumbbell Bench Press (MJ)	5 x 5 at	
Twisting Crunch (ab)	3 x 20	
Back Extension (low back)	3 x 20 at	

Rest Between Sets and Exercises: <u>4 minutes for power cleans, snatch pulls and push jerks, 3 minutes for all other exercises.</u>

Comments: _____

MJ= Multi-Joint Exercise, MJP= Multi-Joint Power Exercise

Figure 10.8. Week one session of strength/power power phase.

Figure 10.9

WEEK FOUR SESSION OF STRENGTH/POWER POWER PHASE

Sport/Activity <u>Strength/Power</u>　　　　　　　　　**Week** <u>4</u>

Training Phase <u>Power</u>　　　　　　　　　　　　**Date** <u>October 26-31</u>

Exercises	Planned Sets x Reps at Weight	Actual Sets x Reps at Weight
Clean Pulls from Floor (MJP)	5 x 2 at	
Snatch Pulls from Knees (MJP)	5 x 3 at	
Push Press (MJP)	5 x 3 at	
Back Squat (MJ)	4 x 3 at	
Twisting Crunch (ab)	3 x 20	

Rest Between Sets and Exercises: <u>4 minutes all exercises.</u>

Comments: <u>Light day, do leg press instead of back squat.</u>

MJ= Multi-Joint Exercise, MJP= Multi-Joint Power Exercise

Figure 10.9. Week four session of strength/power power phase.

The weekly variation of the strength/power peaking phase was outlined in Figure 9.6. A training session for week one of this phase is developed in Figure 10.10. The goal of the peaking phase is to maximize the athlete's strength and power for the competitive season. Therefore, all training sessions in this phase are comprised of predominantly multi-joint power and multi-joint strength-oriented type exercises. The week one session begins with three multi-joint power exercises followed by two multi-joint strength exercises. One of the multi-joint strength exercises is for the lower body (back squat) and one for the upper body (bench press). All these exercises are performed for three sets of three repetitions, with four minutes rest between sets and exercises. The small number of repetitions per set and the relatively long rest periods allow the athlete to use maximal resistances on heavy training days so that maximal strength and power can be developed. If needed, it is possible to vary the exercise choice on light training days to allow the lower back musculature to recover from the heavy training days.

Figure 10.11 spells out a training session for the sixth week of the peaking phase. In order to peak, maximal strength and power, heavy resistances must be utilized. In accordance, the multi-joint power and multi-joint exercises in the sixth week of this phase are performed for only one or two repetitions per set. In addition, long rest periods of four to five minutes between sets and exercises are used so that the athlete can recover sufficiently to use maximal or near-maximal 1 RM resistances. Clean and snatch pulls are performed starting with the bar at knee height rather than on the floor. This starting position mimics closely the initial position from which many strength power athletes develop power within the context of competitive events.

Since the goal of this phase is to peak total body strength/power, single-joint exercises are omitted in the training phase. This is also done to decrease total volume so the athlete can completely recover between resistance training sessions. Complete recovery between sessions is necessary if the athlete is to employ 1 RM or near 1 RM resistances.

Figure 10.10

WEEK ONE SESSION OF STRENGTH/POWER PEAKING PHASE

Sport/Activity Strength/Power   **Week** 1

Training Phase Peaking   **Date** February 14-21

Exercises	Planned Sets x Reps at Weight	Actual Sets x Reps at Weight
Power Cleans from Knees (MJP)	3 x 3 at	
Snatch Pulls from Floor (MJP)	3 x 3 at	
Push Press (MJP)	3 x 3 at	
Back Squat (MJ)	3 x 3 at	
Bench Press (MJ)	3 x 3 at	
Incline Bent Leg Sit-up (ab)	3 x 20	

Rest Between Sets and Exercises: 4 minutes for power cleans and snatch pulls, 3 minutes all others.

Comments: _____

MJ= Multi-Joint Exercise, MJP= Multi-Joint Power Exercise

Figure 10.10. Week one session of strength/power peaking phase.

Figure 10.11

WEEK SIX SESSION OF STRENGTH/POWER PEAKING PHASE

Sport/Activity Strength/Power

Week 4

Training Phase Peaking

Date April 17-13

Exercises	Planned Sets x Reps at Weight	Actual Sets x Reps at Weight
Clean Pulls from Knees (MJP)	3 x 1 at	
Snatch Pulls from Knees (MJP)	3 x 2 at	
Push Jerk (MJP)	3 x 2 at	
Bench Press (MJ)	3 x 1 at	
Twisting Crunch (ab)	3 x 20	

Rest Between Sets and Exercises: 4-5 minutes all exercises.

Comments: Hold weight on chest for crunches to increase resistance as needed.

MJ= Multi-Joint Exercise, MJP= Multi-Joint Power Exercise

Figure 10.11. *Week six session of strength/power peaking phase.*

The strength/power competition phase, weekly variation, was laid out in Figure 9.7. Figure 10.12 depicts a week one training session during the competition phase. The goal of the competition phase is to maintain the strength/power gained during the previous phases. In order to maintain total body strength and power, predominantly multi-joint power and multi-joint strength-oriented exercises are utilized throughout. Training sessions in week one are comprised of three multi-joint power exercises and one multi-joint strength exercise. All exercises are performed for three sets of three repetitions with three to four minutes rest between sets and exercises. This should allow the athlete to utilize very heavy resistances for the desired number of repetitions. Training time during the competitive season is at a premium—therefore, no single-joint exercises are employed during the competition phase, but might be added based on individual needs (such as a previous injury).

Figure 10.13 outlines a training session during the eighth week of the competition phase. The session consists of two multi-joint power exercises and one multi-joint strength exercise, all consisting of three sets of one repetition. All sets should be performed at or near the one repetition maximum for each of the exercises. This gears the peaking of maximal strength and power for the major competitions. In addition, compared to week one, there's a smaller volume of training, which should allow total recovery prior to major competitions. The push jerk is included during the eighth week of the competition phase, as opposed to the push press, which is included during the first week. The push jerk is an exercise that's slightly more power oriented than the push press, and is used near the end of the phase to peak maximal power.

Figure 10.12

WEEK ONE SESSION OF STRENGTH/POWER COMPETITION PHASE

Sport/Activity Strength/Power

Training Phase Competition

Week 1

Date April 14-20

Exercises	Planned Sets x Reps at Weight	Actual Sets x Reps at Weight
Power Clean (MJP)	3 x 3 at	
Snatch Pull from Knees (MJP)	3 x 3 at	
Push Press (MJP)	3 x 3 at	
Squat (MJ)	3 x 3 at	
Crunch (ab)	3 x 20	

Rest Between Sets and Exercises: 3-4 minutes for all exercises.

Comments: _____

MJ= Multi-Joint Exercise, MJP= Multi-Joint Power Exercise

Figure 10.12. Week one session of strength/power competition phase.

Figure 10.13

WEEK EIGHT SESSION OF STRENGTH/POWER COMPETITION PHASE

Sport/Activity Strength/Power

Training Phase Competition

Week 8

Date May 23-29

Exercises	Planned Sets x Reps at Weight	Actual Sets x Reps at Weight
Power Clean from Knees (MJP)	3 x 1 at	
Push Jerk (MJP)	3 x 1 at	
Back Squat (MJ)	3 x 1 at	
Twisting Sit-ups on Incline Board (ab)	3 x 20	

Rest Between Sets and Exercises: 4-5 minutes all exercises.

Comments: _____

MJ= Multi-Joint Exercise, MJP= Multi-Joint Power Exercise

Figure 10.13. Week eight session of strength/power competition phase.

The weekly variation for the basketball hypertrophy training phase was developed in Figure 9.8. A week one training session is seen in Figure 10.14. The session begins with three multi-joint exercises, followed by arm and leg exercises performed in alternating body part sequence. Of course, this type sequence allows more recovery time before training the same body part, as compared to knocking out successive exercises for the same body part. These exercises are performed for three sets of 10 repetitions; except for abdominal exercises, which consist of three sets of 20 reps. The recommended resistance for all exercises should make completion of the desired number of repetitions in all three sets somewhat difficult, especially on those heavy training days. There are three-minute rest periods between sets and exercises. This can be cut down to two minutes after the first week of training if the athlete finds he or she can tolerate shorter rest periods.

A week eight training session for the basketball hypertrophy phase is outlined in Figure 10.15. One difference between the training performed in week eight versus the first week is the addition of a fourth multi-joint exercise. Another difference is the shortening of rest periods to 1.5 minutes. It is also possible throughout the phase to begin to stack exercises for the same body part. A good example of stacking would be performing all leg exercises in sequence, placing greater training stress on the legs than if performing leg exercises, say, in alternating fashion with arm exercises.

Because basketball involves independent action of each arm and leg, it would be desirable in the latter weeks of the phase to incorporate dumbbell and one-legged and one-armed exercises, as opposed to using a barbell or performing the exercises in a two-limb fashion. Throughout the hypertrophy phase, the same weight can be used for all three sets of an exercise. But the resistance should be increased when all three sets can be performed for the desired number of reps on a heavy training day. (Otherwise it wouldn't be a heavy training day, now would it?)

Figure 10.14

WEEK ONE SESSION OF BASKETBALL HYPERTROPHY PHASE

Sport/Activity Basketball   **Week** 1

Training Phase Hypertrophy   **Date** April 1-7

Exercises	Planned Sets x Reps at Weight	Actual Sets x Reps at Weight
Back Squat (MJ)	3 x 10 at	
Bench Press (MJ)	3 x 10 at	
Lat Pulldown (MJ)	3 x 10 at	
Knee Extension (leg)	3 x 10 at	
Knee Curl (leg)	3 x 10 at	
Triceps Pushdown (arm)	3 x 10 at	
Standing Calf Raise (leg)	3 x 10 at	
Elbow Curl (arm)	3 x 10 at	
Hip Abduction-Adduction (leg)	3 x 10 at	
Shoulder Lateral Raise (arm)	3 x 10 at	
Crunch (ab)	3 x 20	

Rest Between Sets and Exercises: 3 minutes all exercises.

Comments: _____

MJ= Multi-Joint Exercise, MJP= Multi-Joint Power Exercise

Figure 10.14. Week one session of basketball hypertrophy phase.

Figure 10.15

WEEK EIGHT SESSION OF BASKETBALL HYPERTROPHY PHASE

Sport/Activity Basketball

Week 8

Training Phase Hypertrophy

Date May 17-23

Exercises	Planned Sets x Reps at Weight	Actual Sets x Reps at Weight
Leg Press (MJ)	3 x 10 at	
Incline Press (MJ)	3 x 10 at	
Lat Pulldown (MJ)	3 x 10 at	
Lunge (MJ)	3 x 10 at	
Standing Knee Curl (leg)	3 x 10 at	
Standing Calf Raise (leg)	3 x 10 at	
Dumbbell Military Press (arm)	3 x 10 at	
Triceps Pushdown (arm)	3 x 10 at	
Back Extension (low back)	3 x 15 at	
Twisting Incline Bent Leg Sit-up (ab)	3 x 20	

Rest Between Sets and Exercises: 1.5 minutes for all exercises.

Comments:

MJ= Multi-Joint Exercise

Figure 10.15. *Week eight session of basketball hypertrophy phase.*

Figure 9.9 developed the weekly variation for the basketball strength phase. A typical training session in week one of the strength phase is outlined in Figure 10.16. The session begins with four multi-joint exercises, followed by two leg and two arm exercises. Lower back exercises and abdominal exercises are saved for last in the training session. All multi-joint and single-joint exercises—except for abdominal and lower back exercise—are performed for four sets of eight repetitions with three minutes rest between sets and exercises.

The resistance used for multi-joint exercises should be increased in each set to the degree that a true eight repetition maximum resistance is used only in the last set of each exercise. To accomplish this, the resistance used in the first set of any exercise should be approximately 85% of the true eight repetition maximum. The resistance is then increased 5% for the next two sets, and 100% of the 8 RM is used in the fourth set on heavy training days. A true eight repetition maximum resistance can be used for all sets of arm and leg exercises. The resistance should be increased for any exercise whenever eight reps can be performed in the fourth set on heavy training days.

A training session from the sixth week of the strength phase appears in Figure 10.17. The session consists primarily of multi-joint and multi-joint power exercises. Multi-joint power exercises are tackled first in the session, followed by multi-joint, ab, and lower back exercises. All multi-joint power and multi-joint exercises are performed for three sets of six repetitions. The resistance utilized for these exercises during the first, second, and third set should be approximately 90, 95, and 100% of the 6 RM. Resistance should be increased whenever six repetitions can be performed during the third set of a particular exercise. The allotted rest time is three minutes between all sets and exercises. If tolerated by the trainee, the rest between sets and exercises can be decreased when performing the abdominal and lower back exercises.

Figure 10.16

WEEK ONE SESSION OF BASKETBALL STRENGTH PHASE

Sport/Activity Basketball

Week 1

Training Phase Strength

Date May 24-30

Exercises	Planned Sets x Reps at Weight	Actual Sets x Reps at Weight
Back Squat (MJ)	4 x 8 at	
Bench Press (MJ)	4 x 8 at	
T Bar Row (MJ)	4 x 8 at	
Behind Neck Press (MJ)	4 x 8 at	
Knee Curl (leg)	4 x 8 at	
Standing Calf Raise (leg)	4 x 8 at	
Elbow Curl (arm)	4 x 8 at	
Wrist Curl (arm)	4 x 8 at	
Good Mornings (low back)	3 x 15 at	
Crunches (ab)	3 x 20	

Rest Between Sets and Exercises: 3 minutes for all exercises.

Comments:

MJ= Multi-Joint Exercise

Figure 10.16. Week one session of basketball strength phase.

Figure 10.17

WEEK SIX SESSION OF BASKETBALL STRENGTH PHASE

Sport/Activity Basketball   **Week** 6

Training Phase Strength   **Date** June 28 - July 4

Exercises	Planned Sets x Reps at Weight	Actual Sets x Reps at Weight
Clean Pull from Knees (MJP)	3 x 6 at	
Push Press (MJP)	3 x 6 at	
Leg Press (MJ)	3 x 6 at	
Dumbbell Bench Press (MJ)	3 x 6 at	
Lat Pulldown (MJ)	3 x 6 at	
Knee Curl (leg)	3 x 8 at	
Standing Calf Raise (leg)	3 x 8 at	
Triceps Pushdown (arm)	3 x 8 at	
Wrist Curl (arm)	3 x 8 at	
Rotatory Torso (ab)	3 x 15	
Crunches (ab)	3 x 20	

Rest Between Sets and Exercises: 3 minutes for all exercises.

Comments:

MJ= Multi-Joint Exercise, MJP= Multi-Joint Power Exercise

Figure 10.17. Week six session of basketball strength phase.

Figure 9.10 contains the weekly variation of the basketball training power phase. A typical week one training session is layed out in Figure 10.18. The session begins with two multiple-joint power exercises. One of these exercises uses dumbbells because, as mentioned, it is important for the arms of a basketball player to act independently. The power-oriented exercises are followed by three multi-joint exercises, one of which is again dumbbell oriented. Multi-joint exercises are followed by two arm exercises, including the wrist roller, because grip and forearm strength are important for performance in basketball. The training session ends with two twisting type abdominal exercises.

Power-oriented exercises are performed for four sets of five repetitions; multi-joint exercises for four sets of six repetitions. Arm and abdominal exercises are de-emphasized slightly during the power phase, with only three sets. On heavy training days, the first, second, third, and fourth sets of power-oriented exercises should be performed at 85, 90, 95 and 100% of the five repetition maximum for lifts. This same pattern of increasing resistance should be followed when performing multi-joint exercises.

Resistance for the multi-joint power and multi-joint exercises is increased slightly when the desired number of reps can be performed for all four sets. On heavy training days, the resistance used for the remaining exercises in the session should be approximately 95% of the rep max.

A session for week four of the power training phase is developed in Figure 10.19. The session consists exclusively of multi-joint power and multi-joint exercises, except for one abdominal exercise. Power-oriented exercises are emphasized, with four sets of each, and only three sets of multi-joint and abdominal exercises. Training volume is quite low during this last week of the power phase, with only three reps per set. However, on heavy training days, the weight used for each set should range between 90-100% of the 3 RM. Essentially, the goal should be to come as close to the 3 RM as possible, and yet be able to perform three repetitions for each of the sets. Long rest periods of four minutes between sets/exercises should allow the athlete time for enough recovery to stay within the 90-100% range of the 3 RM.

Two of the multi-joint power exercises utilize a dumbbell instead of a barbell. This is done for several reasons. When performing the dumbbell push jerk, each arm acts independently. When performing the dumbbell one-arm snatch, the use of a dumbbell and a lighter weight will not only allow the athlete to utilize one arm at a time, but also to move at a faster speed, which is similar to what must be done when on the basketball court.

Figure 10.18

WEEK ONE SESSION OF BASKETBALL POWER PHASE

Sport/Activity __Basketball__   Week __1__

Training Phase __Power__   Date __July 5-11__

Exercises	Planned Sets x Reps at Weight	Actual Sets x Reps at Weight
Clean Pull from Floor (MJP)	4 x 5 at	
Dumbbell Push Press (MJP)	4 x 5 at	
Back Squat (MJ)	4 x 6 at	
Dumbbell Bench Press (MJ)	4 x 6 at	
Lat Pulldown (MJ)	4 x 6 at	
Standing Elbow Curl (arm)	3 x 6 at	
Wrist Roller (arm)	3 x 6 at	
Rotatory Torso (ab)	3 x 10 at	
Twisting Crunch (ab)	3 x 20	

Rest Between Sets and Exercises: __3 minutes for MJP & MJ, 2 minutes all others.__

Comments: _____

MJ= Multi-Joint Exercise, MJP= Multi-Joint Power Exercise

Figure 10.18. Week one session of basketball power phase.

Figure 10.19

WEEK FOUR SESSION OF BASKETBALL POWER PHASE

Sport/Activity Basketball

Week 4

Training Phase Power

Date July 26-August 1

Exercises	Planned Sets x Reps at Weight	Actual Sets x Reps at Weight
Snatch Pull from Knees (MJP)	4 x 3 at	
Dumbbell Push Jerk (MJP)	4 x 3 at	
One Arm Dumbbell Snatch (MJP)	4 x 3 at	
Leg Press (MJ)	3 x 3 at	
Dumbbell Bench Press (MJ)	3 x 3 at	
Rotatory Torso (ab)	3 x 15	

Rest Between Sets and Exercises: 3 minutes all.

Comments:

MJ= Multi-Joint Exercise, MJP= Multi-Joint Power Exercise

Figure 10.19. Week four session of basketball power phase.

For a look at the weekly variation of the basketball recovery phase, check Figure 9.11. Then check Figure 10.20 for our breakdown of a week one session. Although the recovery phase is supposed to promote physiological/psychological surcease from prior training phases, for a competitive athlete, this phase should not be an excuse to allow deconditioning to take place. Bearing that in mind, we've included one multi-joint power exercise. Also included in the training session is one upper body and lower body multi-joint exercise. The leg press and dumbbell bent-over row exercises have been chosen because they will result in less lower back stress than an exercise such as squats or barbell bent-over rows. Less stress on the lower back will allow recovery from previous training phases in preparation for the upcoming competitive season.

All the exercises in the session are arranged in a sequence such that no one body part or muscle group is trained twice in succession. This will result in a less stressful regimen than stacking exercises. The multi-joint power and multi-joint exercises should be done in a set repetition format, while the rest of the exercises can be performed in either a set repetition format or a circuit format. Three minutes rest are allowed between sets of multi-joint power exercises; two minutes rest between all other sets and exercises. The same resistance should be used for all sets of an exercise and should be chosen so that the desired number of reps can be performed.

A week two recovery phase session is presented in Figure 10.21. The major difference between the week two session and the week one session is the inclusion of three multi-joint exercises instead of two. In addition, the multi-joint exercises are performed for two sets of 10 repetitions rather than three sets of 10 reps, reducing the total training volume and, therefore, allowing more recovery prior to competition. Akin to week one, multi-joint power and multi-joint exercises should be performed in a set repetition format, while the remainder of exercises can be performed in either a set rep or circuit format. The resistance rationale stays the same from week one to week two.

Figure 10.20

WEEK ONE SESSION OF BASKETBALL RECOVERY PHASE

Sport/Activity Basketball

Week 1

Training Phase Recovery

Date August 2-8

Exercises	Planned Sets x Reps at Weight	Actual Sets x Reps at Weight
Snatch Pull from Knees (MJP)	3 x 6 at	
Bench Press (MJ)	3 x 10 at	
Leg Press (MJ)	3 x 10 at	
Dumbbell Bent Over Row (arm)	2 x 12 at	
Knee Curl (leg)	2 x 12 at	
Elbow Curl (arm)	2 x 12 at	
Hip Adduction/Abduction (leg)	2 x 12 at	
Crunch (ab)	2 x 20	
Back Extensions (low back)	2 x 15 at	
Sit-ups on Incline Board (ab)	2 x 20	

Rest Between Sets and Exercises: 3 minutes MJP, 2 minutes all others.

Comments: _____

MJ= Multi-Joint Exercise, MJP= Multi-Joint Power Exercise

Figure 10.20. Week one session of basketball recovery phase.

Figure 10.21

WEEK TWO SESSION OF BASKETBALL RECOVERY PHASE

Sport/Activity Basketball   **Week** 2

Training Phase Recovery   **Date** August 9-15

Exercises	Planned Sets x Reps at Weight	Actual Sets x Reps at Weight
Push Press (MJP)	3 x 6 at	
Leg Press (MJ)	2 x 10 at	
Bench Press (MJ)	2 x 10 at	
Lat Pulldown (MJ)	2 x 10 at	
Knee Curl (leg)	2 x 10 at	
Hip Adduction/Abduction (leg)	2 x 10 at	
Elbow Curl (arm)	2 x 10 at	
Crunch (ab)	2 x 20	
Back Extension (low back)	2 x 15 at	

Rest Between Sets and Exercises: 3 minutes MJP, 2 minutes all others.

Comments:

MJ= Multi-Joint Exercise, MJP= Multi-Joint Power Exercise

Figure 10.21. Week two session of basketball recovery phase.

Figure 10.22 spins off a single basketball in-season training session from the weekly model seen in Figure 9.12. The session consists primarily of multi-joint exercises. This is because training time during an in-season period is at a real premium. Utilizing multi-joint exercises optimizes and shortens the time spent in the weight room in-season. The exercises are chosen such that all of the major muscle groups do receive some training stimulus during each session. Resistance should be determined so that the desired number of repetitions per set can be performed for all three sets. If the time dedicated to resistance training needs to be further shortened in-season, two instead of three sets of each exercise can be done.

Figure 10.23 presents an in-season concentrated load training session. This type session could be ideal during an in-season week in which no games are played, or two to three weeks prior to the start of a tournament. The goal of the concentrated load session is to regain and peak strength/power. Differing from the normal in-season training session, two multi-joint power exercises are employed instead of one. Even in a week in which no games are played, training time is at a premium. Therefore, the training session will still consist of multi-joint exercises instead of single-joint ones to minimize time in the weight room. Resistance for the multi-joint power exercises should be chosen so that six repetitions can be completed for all three sets of each exercise. However, the resistance used on heavy training days for the other multi-joint exercises for sets one, two, and three should be 90, 95 and 100% of the eight repetition maximum per exercise—so that there is a stimulus to actually increase strength during a week in which a concentrated load is used.

Figure 10.22

NORMAL WEEK SESSION OF BASKETBALL IN-SEASON PHASE

Sport/Activity Basketball

Week Normal In-Season

Training Phase In-Scason

Date December 15-March 30

Exercises	Planned Sets x Reps at Weight	Actual Sets x Reps at Weight
Dumbbell Push Jerk (MJP)	3 x 6 at	
Leg Press (MJ)	3 x 8 at	
Bench Press (MJ)	3 x 8 at	
Lat Pulldown (MJ)	3 x 8 at	
Dip (MJ)	3 x 8	
Crunch (ab)	3 x 20	
Back Extension (low back)	3 x 15 at	

Rest Between Sets and Exercises: 2 minutes all exercises.

Comments:

MJ= Multi-Joint Exercise, MJP= Multi-Joint Power Exercise

Figure 10.22. Normal week session of basketball in-season phase.

Figure 10.23

CONCENTRATED LOAD SESSION OF BASKETBALL IN-SEASON PHASE

Sport/Activity Basketball

Week 2-3 Weeks Prior to Start of Tournaments

Training Phase In-Season

Date April 1-8

Exercises	Planned Sets x Reps at Weight	Actual Sets x Reps at Weight
One Arm Dumbbell Snatch (MJP)	3 x 6 at	
Dumbbell Push Jerk (MJP)	3 x 6 at	
Back Squat (MJ)	3 x 8 at	
Bench Press (MJ)	3 x 8 at	
Lat Pulldown (MJ)	3 x 8 at	
Dumbbell Overhead Press (MJ)	3 x 8 at	
Crunch (ab)	3 x 20	

Rest Between Sets and Exercises: 3 minutes MJP, 2 minutes MJ.

Comments: _____

MJ= Multi-Joint Exercise, MJP= Multi-Joint Power Exercise

Figure 10.23. Concentrated load session of basketball in-season phase.

GENERAL FITNESS TRAINING PLAN

The hypertrophy I phase of the general fitness program was developed in Figure 9.13. A week one training session is further developed in Figure 10.24. The exercises are arranged in an alternating muscle group or body part fashion to allow sufficient recovery. Exercises are chosen such that all major muscle groups receive a training stimulus from at least one exercise. For the true beginner, all of the exercises can be performed using resistance training machines rather than free weights. This will facilitate the learning of proper technique. As the trainee becomes proficient with exercise technique, free weight type exercises can be substituted if desired. Initially, resistance should be chosen such that 20 repetitions per set can be performed in relatively easy fashion. This will help minimize muscular soreness. Over time, resistance can be gradually increased.

A week four training session of the hypertrophy I phase can be seen in Figure 10.25. The major differences between the week four session and the week one session: greater training volume (more exercises, three sets instead of one), and shorter rest periods between sets and exercises. Resistances in week four should be greater than in week one, since there are 15 instead of 20 reps per set, and by this time the trainee should be experiencing an increase in muscular strength. The same resistance for all three sets of an exercise can be utilized, but should be such that completion of the desired number of repetitions in the third set is difficult.

If you're tolerating the training stress, it is possible to begin to stack exercises for the same body part, instead of alternating. Exercises can be done in either a set repetition or a circuit format, depending on the preference of the trainee. If you find yourself not tolerating the one-minute rest periods between sets and exercises, a slightly longer time can be utilized, or the rest period can be allowed to gradually lengthen as the training session progresses (e.g., first set one minute, if done in a circuit fashion; 2nd set one-and-a-half minutes; 3rd set two minutes).

Figure 10.24

WEEK ONE SESSION OF GENERAL FITNESS HYPERTROPHY I PHASE

Sport/Activity General Fitness

Week 1

Training Phase Hypertrophy I

Date January 1-7

Exercises	Planned Sets x Reps at Weight	Actual Sets x Reps at Weight
Leg Press (MJ)	1 x 20 at	
Bench Press (MJ)	1 x 20 at	
Lat Pulldown (MJ)	1 x 20 at	
Knee Curl (leg)	1 x 20 at	
Elbow Curl (arm)	1 x 20 at	
Knee Extension (leg)	1 x 20 at	
Elbow Extension (arm)	1 x 20 at	
Crunch (ab)	1 x 20 at	

Rest Between Sets and Exercises: 3 minutes all exercises.

Comments: Concentrate on correct exercise technique.

MJ= Multi-Joint Exercise, MJP= Multi-Joint Power Exercise

Figure 10.24. Week one session of general fitness hypertrophy I phase.

Figure 10.25

WEEK FOUR SESSION OF GENERAL FITNESS HYPERTROPHY I PHASE

Sport/Activity General Fitness   **Week** 4

Training Phase Hypertrophy I   **Date** January 25-31

Exercises	Planned Sets x Reps at Weight	Actual Sets x Reps at Weight
Leg Press (MJ)	3 x 15 at	
Bench Press (MJ)	3 x 15 at	
Lat Pulldown (MJ)	3 x 15 at	
Knee Curl (leg)	3 x 15 at	
Elbow Curl (arm)	3 x 15 at	
Knee Extension (leg)	3 x 15 at	
Elbow Extension (arm)	3 x 15 at	
Calf Raise (leg)	3 x 15 at	
Shoulder Lateral Raise (arm)	3 x 15 at	
Hip Adduction/Abduction (leg)	3 x 15 at	
Back Extension (low back)	3 x 15 at	
Crunch (ab)	3 x 20	

Rest Between Sets and Exercises: 1 minute all exercises.

Comments: _____

MJ= Multi-Joint Exercise

Figure 10.25. Week four session of general fitness hypertrophy I phase.

Figure 9.14 shows the weekly variation for the hypertrophy II phase. In Figure 10.26, a week one session of the hypertrophy II phase is developed more fully. There are an equal number of upper and lower body exercises, and all exercises require the same number of sets. Total training volume is quite high in this session: four sets of 15 reps, except for the abdominal exercise (four sets of 20 reps).

The calf raise is performed after the bench press in order to allow some recovery of the upper body prior to the performance of the next two multi-joint upper body exercises. In general, the exercises are arranged in alternating body part/muscle group order so that some recovery is allowed. The rest period of two minutes may be lengthened toward the end of the session if the trainee is "losing it"; or shortened if the trainee is tolerating the two-minute rests very well.

A week four session for the hypertrophy II phase is expanded and developed in Figure 10.27. This training session places a greater emphasis on the upper body. The session begins with multi-joint exercises. Then all upper body exercises are performed in sequence immediately thereafter. Lower body exercises are saved for last. Upper body exercises are performed for five sets of 15 repetitions; lower body for three sets of 15 repetitions. This is clearly indicative of the session's emphasis on the upper body. On heavy training days throughout this phase, a 15 RM resistance for the desired number of repetitions should be used for all three sets of an exercise.

Figure 10.26

WEEK ONE SESSION OF GENERAL FITNESS HYPERTROPHY II PHASE

Sport/Activity General Fitness

Week 1

Training Phase Hypertrophy II

Date February 1-7

Exercises	Planned Sets x Reps at Weight	Actual Sets x Reps at Weight
Leg Press (MJ)	4 x 15 at	
Bench Press (MJ)	4 x 15 at	
Calf Raise (leg)	4 x 15 at	
Seated Overhead Press (MJ)	4 x 15 at	
Lat Pulldown (MJ)	4 x 15 at	
Knee Curl (leg)	4 x 15 at	
Elbow Curl (arm)	4 x 15 at	
Knee Extension (leg)	4 x 15 at	
Elbow Extension (arm)	4 x 15 at	
Hip Adduction/Abduction (leg)	4 x 15 at	
Flyes (arm)	4 x 15 at	
Twisting Crunch (ab)	4 x 20	

Rest Between Sets and Exercises: 2 minutes all exercises.

Comments:

MJ= Multi-Joint Exercise

Figure 10.26. Week one session of general fitness hypertrophy II phase

Figure 10.27

WEEK FOUR SESSION OF GENERAL FITNESS HYPERTROPHY II PHASE

Sport/Activity <u>General Fitness</u>   **Week** <u>4</u>

Training Phase <u>Hypertrophy II</u>   **Date** <u>February 22-28</u>

Exercises	Planned Sets x Reps at Weight	Actual Sets x Reps at Weight
Leg Press (MJ)	4 x 12 at	
Bench Press (MJ)	4 x 12 at	
Lunge (MJ)	4 x 12 at	
Seated Overhead Press (MJ)	4 x 12 at	
Seated Row (arm)	5 x 15 at	
Upright Row (arm)	5 x 15 at	
Triceps Pushdown (arm)	5 x 15 at	
Dumbbell Concentration Curl (arm)	5 x 15 at	
Bent Leg Sit-ups on Incline Board (ab)	5 x 15	
Back Extension (low back)	5 x 15 at	
Knee Curl (leg)	3 x 15 at	
Calf Raise (leg)	3 x 15 at	
Hip Adduction/Abduction (leg)	3 x 15 at	

Rest Between Sets and Exercises: <u>2 minutes for MJ, 1 minute for SJ.</u>

Comments: _____

MJ= Multi-Joint Exercise, SJ=Single-Joint Exercise

Figure 10.27. Week four session of general fitness hypertrophy II phase.

The weekly variation of the hypertrophy/strength phase was developed in Figure 9.15. A more specific week one session is seen in Figure 10.28. Here's a session that places emphasis on upper body hypertrophy/strength. Upper body multi-joint exercises are tackled first—four sets of 10 repetitions. Lower body multi-joint exercises are done for three sets of 10 repetitions. Upper body single-joint exercises, done prior to lower body single-joint exercises, consume four sets of 12 reps per exercise. Upper body single-joint exercises are performed for three sets of 12 reps.

If the desire is to emphasize strength to a slightly greater extent, rest periods for multi-joint exercises can be lengthened from three to four minutes. The added recovery time will allow the trainee to utilize slightly greater resistances.

On heavy training days, resistances used for upper body multi-joint exercises should follow a pattern of 85, 90, 95 and 100% of the 10 RM for the first, second, third and fourth sets. Upper body single-joint exercises will follow a similar pattern, except the resistance is based upon the 12 RM. On heavy training days, resistance used for the lower body multi-joint exercises should follow a pattern of 90, 95 and 100% of the 10 RM for the first, second, and third sets. The lower body single-joint exercises would follow a similar pattern, except the resistance would be based on the 12 repetition maximum.

A week four session for the hypertrophy/strength phase is developed in Figure 10.29. This session emphasizes total body strength. Multi-joint exercises are performed first for four sets of 10 repetitions. Single-joint upper and lower body exercises come after multi-joint, for only three sets of 12 reps. The exception is the abdominal exercise, which is performed for three sets of 20 repetitions. On heavy training days, the resistance used in the first, second, third, and fourth sets of the multi-joint exercises should follow a pattern of 90, 95, 100, and 100% of the 10 RM for the given exercise. This may mean you won't be able to perform 10 reps during the third and fourth sets. However, you should strive to perform as many repetitions as possible. A 12 RM resistance should be used for all three sets of upper and lower body single-joint exercises. Again, this may mean that the trainee can't perform 12 repetitions in all of the sets. However, he or she should strive to perform as many reps as possible, in the second and third sets especially.

Figure 10.28

WEEK ONE SESSION OF GENERAL FITNESS HYPERTROPHY STRENGTH PHASE

Sport/Activity General Fitness

Week 1

Training Phase Hypertrophy/Strength

Date March 1-7

Exercises	Planned Sets x Reps at Weight	Actual Sets x Reps at Weight
Bench Press (MJ)	4 x 10 at	
T Bar Row (MJ)	4 x 10 at	
Hip Sled (MJ)	3 x 10 at	
Leg Press (MJ)	3 x 10 at	
Elbow Curl (arm)	4 x 12 at	
Upright Row (arm)	4 x 12 at	
Knee Curl (leg)	3 x 12 at	
Donkey Calf Raise (leg)	3 x 12 at	
Weighted Incline Bent Leg Sit-up (ab)	4 x 20	

Rest Between Sets and Exercises: 2 minutes for MJ, 1 minute for SJ.

Comments:

MJ= Multi-Joint Exercise, SJ= Single-Joint Exercise

Figure 10.28. Week one session of general fitness hypertrophy/strength phase.

Figure 10.29

WEEK FOUR SESSION OF GENERAL FITNESS HYPERTROPHY STRENGTH PHASE

Sport/Activity General Fitness

Week 4

Training Phase Hypertrophy Strength

Date March 25-31

Exercises	Planned Sets x Reps at Weight	Actual Sets x Reps at Weight
Hip Sled (MJ)	4 x 10 at	
Bench Press (MJ)	4 x 10 at	
Leg Press (MJ)	4 x 10 at	
T Bar Row (MJ)	4 x 10 at	
Dumbbell Standing Elbow Curl (arm)	3 x 12 at	
Standing Knee Curl (leg)	3 x 12 at	
Upright Row (arm)	3 x 12 at	
Inclined Bent Leg Sit-up (ab)	3 x 20	

Rest Between Sets and Exercises: 2 minutes for MJ, 1 minute for SJ.

Comments: _____

MJ= Multi-Joint Exercise, SJ= Single-Joint Exercise

Figure 10.29. Week four session of general fitness hypertrophy/strength phase.

Study Figure 9.16 for the weekly variation of the general fitness strength phase. A week one session of the strength phase can be further studied in Figure 10.30. This session emphasizes lower body strength. Therefore, the lower body multi-joint exercises are performed first and are immediately followed by the one lower body single-joint exercise (calf raises). Lower body multi-joint and lower body single-joint exercises are all performed for four sets of eight repetitions. All upper body exercises are performed for three sets of eight reps. The resistance utilized for all exercises in this session—except the abdominal exercise—should be 100% of the 8 RM for that exercise. This could mean that during the third and fourth sets it may not be possible for the trainee to knock out the indicated eight reps. However, as should always be the case, the trainee should strive to perform as many repetitions as possible.

Figure 10.31 further delineates a week four session of the general fitness strength phase. This training interlude emphasizes lower body and bench press strength. The bench press is performed for five sets of six repetitions, and falls first in the session. Bench press is followed by both of the multi-joint lower body exercises (five sets of six repetitions). The two multi-joint upper body exercises are performed for three sets of six repetitions later in the session.

The resistance used for exercises performed for five sets should follow a pattern of 90-95% of the six repetition max for the first and second sets. The third, fourth, and fifth sets are all done using 100% of the 6 RM. Even with the four-minute rest periods permitted between sets and exercises, it may not be possible to perform six repetitions in all of these sets. The trainee should, as always, strive to push out as many reps as possible in the third, fourth, and fifth sets. The resistance utilized for the multi-joint exercises performed for three sets should follow a pattern of 90, 95, 100% of the 6 RM, with the trainee striving to perform as many repetitions as possible in the third set. Crunches should be worked utilizing a weight that allows approximately 20 repetitions per set.

Figure 10.30

WEEK ONE SESSION OF GENERAL FITNESS STRENGTH PHASE

Sport/Activity General Fitness

Week 1

Training Phase Strength

Date April 1-7

Exercises	Planned Sets x Reps at Weight	Actual Sets x Reps at Weight
Hip Sled (MJ)	4 x 8 at	
Leg Press (MJ)	4 x 8 at	
Calf Raise (leg)	4 x 8 at	
Bench Press (MJ)	3 x 8 at	
Seated Row (MJ)	3 x 8 at	
Overhead Press (MJ)	3 x 8 at	
Elbow Curl (arm)	3 x 8 at	
Crunch (ab)	3 x 20	

Rest Between Sets and Exercises: 3 minutes for MJ, 2 minutes for SJ.

Comments:

MJ= Multi-Joint Exercise, SJ= Single-Joint Exercise

Figure 10.30. Week one session of general fitness strength phase.

Figure 10.31

WEEK FOUR SESSION OF GENERAL FITNESS STRENGTH PHASE

Sport/Activity General Fitness   **Week** 4

Training Phase Strength   **Date** April 24-30

Exercises	Planned Sets x Reps at Weight	Actual Sets x Reps at Weight
Bench Press (MJ)	5 x 6 at	
Hip Sled (MJ)	5 x 6 at	
Leg Press (MJ)	5 x 6 at	
Seated Row (MJ)	3 x 6 at	
Overhead Press (MJ)	3 x 6 at	
Weighted Crunch (ab)	3 x 20	

Rest Between Sets and Exercises: 4 minutes all exercises.

Comments:

MJ= Multi-Joint Exercise

Figure 10.31. Week four session of general fitness strength phase.

You should now have an excellent idea of periodized resistance training concepts, and be able to design programs to meet the needs of anyone, especially yourself. The key to designing optimal periodized resistance training programs is to manipulate all of the training variables to meet the needs of the trainee. Creativity in changing the program and the knowledge you have gained from this book will allow you to design optimal programs.

Here's another key to success: if a program is not working, do not be afraid to evaluate it and make appropriate changes before you have wasted weeks of training time.

Take all the information presented and apply it to your own situation in an intelligent manner. If you do so, you will be amazed at the progress you can make in several weeks—and that progress will continue throughout years of training.

Best of luck in designing these optimal periodized programs! You've never felt—or looked—better!

glossary

Active rest phase. A period of light training where the goal is to recover physically and mentally from previous training.

Alternate arm or leg training. Weight training where one repetition is performed with the right arm or leg, and then one with the left arm or leg, before returning to the right arm/leg, and so on.

Barbell. Free weight consisting of a long bar on which weight plates are placed, and which is normally lifted with both arms.

Circuit training. A training method where you move in succession from one exercise to another, with the aim of improving cardiovascular conditioning and bolstering muscular endurance. The trainee might utilize preset strength-training machines to facilitate swift transitions from one exercise to another. Would usually involve moderate weight and relatively high reps. The trainee has the option of repeating the circuit one or more times.

Competition phase. European terminology referring to in-season training.

Competition-specific training. Drills or activities that mimic an actual game or contest, such as a practice game.

Concentric action. Commonly termed "positive work." Development of force while a muscle shortens, such as when lifting a weight in resistance exercises.

Detraining. The deterioration of fitness gains towards untrained levels when training is stopped.

Dumbbell. Free weight made up of a short handle on which weight plates are placed; normally lifted with one arm.

Eccentric action. Commonly termed "negative work." Development of force while a muscle lengthens, as when lowering a weight in most resistance exercises.

First transition. European terminology referring to the late pre-season. The transition from general pre-season training to in-season training.

Force-velocity curve. A graph depicting the maximal tension muscle can generate at several speeds of movement. The slower the speed, the more tension the muscle generates.

General training. Conditioning to develop all-around fitness; not fitness-specific to a given sport.

Growth hormone. Substance produced by the anterior pituitary that in part controls muscle growth and the metabolism of fats and carbohydrates.

Hypertrophy. An increase in muscle size.

Hypertrophy phase. Training period where the major goal is to increase muscle size or mass.

Individualization principle. Idea that a fitness program is optimized by designing it to meet the needs and goals of a specific person.

In-season. Portion of the training year that starts with the first competition and ends with the last competition.

Intensity. A measure of how difficult training is. In weight training, it is defined as a percent of the maximal weight that can be lifted for a specified number of repetitions.

Isometric action. Development of muscle force with no visible movement occurring at a joint.

Lactate. A by-product of deriving energy by burning carbohydrates via anaerobic metabolism. It is in part responsible for the development of fatigue.

Macrocycle. One entire training year, normally thought of as starting with the last competition of one year and ending with the last competition of the following year.

Microcycle. One week of training.

Mesocycle. Referring to a major training phase within a year; or, a training phase four to six weeks in length.

Multi-joint exercise. Weight training exercise where movement takes place at more than one joint, and therefore involves more than one muscle group. Examples are the squat and bench press.

Negative work. Development of force while a muscle lengthens, such as when lowering a weight in most resistance exercises. See **Eccentric action.**

Off-season. Portion of a training year that starts after the last competition of the year and ends when training for the next year's competitions begins.

One repetition maximum (1 RM). Greatest amount of weight that can be lifted for one complete repetition of a particular exercise.

Overload principle. Idea that in order to make fitness gains the body needs to be stressed beyond what it can now comfortably do.

Peaking phase. Training period where the goal is to maximize the ability to perform a certain sport or activity.

Periodization. Planned, variegated training program where changes are made to ensure long-term fitness gains.

Plyometrics. Originally developed by Russian sport scientists in the 1960s, these types of exercises work the neuromuscular system to develop both strength and speed. Examples include the vertical jump, box jumps, and throwing a medicine ball.

Positive work. Development of force while a muscle shortens, such as when lifting a weight in most resistance exercises. See **Concentric action.**

Power exercise. An exercise where it is necessary to move the resistance quickly to do a repetition. Examples are variations of the clean and snatch, and maximal vertical jumps.

Power phase. Training period where the major goal is to increase the rate of force development of the muscles, or increase muscle power.

Preparation phase. European terminology referring to early pre-season. Training at this point is normally aimed at improving basic physical conditioning for the next competitive season.

Pre-season. Portion of a training year beginning when serious preparation for the year's competitions start. Ends with the first competition.

Priority system. Exercise order which stresses major training goals. Exercises relating to such goals would be performed early in the session. For example, if arm size is paramount, you'd give precedence to arm exercises.

Pyramid training. Method of training using progressively heavier or lighter weights and descending/ascending repetitions for an exercise. Essentially, a decreasing number of repetitions per set, with increasing weight; followed by an increase in the number of repetitions, with a decrease in weight.

Repetition. One complete performance of an exercise, usually involving both a lifting and a lowering of the weight.

Repetition maximum (RM). Greatest amount of weight that can be lifted for a specified number of repetitions. For example, a 10 RM is a weight that can be lifted for 10 complete repetitions, but not eleven.

Rest period. Amount of time allowed between sets and exercises in a training session.

Rest principle. Idea that sufficient recovery must be allowed if optimal fitness gains are to occur.

Second transition. European terminology referring to off-season training.

Set. Group of repetitions performed in succession, after which a brief rest is taken.

Set repetition scheme (format). Refers to the number of sets and repetitions performed during training sessions within a designated phase. Normally expressed as a range (e.g., 3-5 sets, 8-10 reps).

Single-joint exercise. Weight training exercise where movement takes place at only one joint, and therefore predominantly involves one muscle group.

Specificity principle. Idea that fitness gains are specific to such things as the muscle groups exercised, or the speed at which the exercise is performed.

Sport-specific training. Conditioning or skill drills aimed at developing the ability to perform a certain sport or activity.

Stacking. Exercise order where more than one exercise for the same muscle group is performed in succession. For example, concentration curls followed by arm curls on a machine.

Strength phase. Training period where the major goal is to increase maximal muscle force.

Testosterone. Male sex hormone produced by the testes.

Training log. Written record of training performance.

Training zone. The desired number of repetitions plus or minus two repetitions. For example, if the program calls for three sets of 10 reps, and you actually do 10, nine and eight reps, you are still within your desired "zone."

Variation principle. Idea that variety and changes in training—such as weight used, or length of the rest period between sets of an exercise—are needed to bring about optimal fitness gains.

Volume. A measure of how much training is performed. In weight training, it is defined as the total number of repetitions, or the total amount of weight lifted in a specified period of time (such as a week).